Church in a Blues Bar

Listening to Hear

Church in a Blues Bar

Listening to Hear

Allan Dayhoff, D. Min.

Evangelize Today
2015

March 2015

ISBN 978-1-312-90706-5

Preface

Something primordial has changed in our time, world, and culture, as it relates to the church and to building faith-bridges to the faith-skeptical. But something else has stayed the same, in the timeless truths of the Gospel, a time-tested invitation that can be accessed by the common man — and by the very common man. Jesus said, "Behold I stand at the door and knock." How and where is He knocking?

I invite you to take a risk with me, to ponder the thoughts we share together, to embrace, question, or reject these words. I hope you will give them honest mindshare — test them in the field as well as in the church.

I have spent my life serving in the church, and I believe the core truths of the Christian faith are as real and true today as ever. But we seem to have lost our stride with evangelism, with sharing our faith, and with knowing just where and how the unchurched think, hunt, suffer, or hide.

Dance studios talk about "dancing in the wild." That does not mean wild dancing — it means taking what you have practiced in the dance studio and trying it out on a regular dance floor, maybe in some restaurant or bar with regular people. Some of the thoughts in this book take the opposite path: the ideas sprang up from being out in the world — "in the wild" — and then I had the wild idea to bring them back to the comfortable studio of the church. My heart is for you to love the studio, but also to take your own adventure into the wild, allowing listening to create *hearing*.

Is the Age of the Church over, for Western culture? Or, for a new generation of seekers, has it maybe just begun?

As a church planter in the 1990s, having our own building was my dream. If we build it, they will come! A place for everyone to call home. I prayed for this final resting place to let our parishioners use their Ministry gifts, a place to develop a loving ethos to grow through Christ. At last, we opened the doors of our 5 million dollar campus, and our building was indeed full.

But "full" was not really *full*. Our church was full of folks who had transferred from the struggling churches all around us. But who else should we be welcoming? What happened to "Knowing Jesus and making Him known?"

The dream changed now. The pathway God had laid before me disappeared into a fog and I became lost and numb, fighting an internal battle with anger and cynicism. I prayed over and over again, "God, do something — I'm dying here."

And now new doors opened, as the old path disappeared for good. I became a nomad once again, not voluntarily, and I found a new group of other lost nomads. I think of them as my "Blues People." At first, they were just people who, like me, enjoy blues music. As I got to know some of them, I prayed for them, and it changed me. My new discoveries brought fire back into my soul for the ministry.

We need to ask ourselves a question: How far away from us is the closest non-Christian life? The non-Christian used to be a neighbor, a friend, and a possible sympathizer to the Christian walk. Things have changed. Sympathy is hard to find. The non-Christians around us are as distant as if they were aborigines, far from the message of the church. But they may be closer to thinking about the eternal Gospel questions than we could imagine. Maybe what we need is a new "starting place." Maybe it takes a new kind of adventurer — researcher, missionary — to find our aborigines: to find a shared language, to hear and understand them.

If the fish are not coming to us, *we must go to them*. How will we do that?

Contents

Chapter 1

Listening in a Blues Bar

Be gracious to me, O Lord, for I am pining away;
Heal me, O Lord, for my bones are dismayed.

Psalm 6:2

I was driving home in October, 2012, on the familiar — but also emotional — trip from my church, six miles away. Things were not well in my head and my heart, and my soul was the traffic cop trying to make sense of the congestion. Tired questions took up too much room inside of me. I heard myself asking, "Does anyone know what it's like to carry a parish around in your head all the time?" My brain felt like a Nascar race on TV, engines roaring around the same old track. Whew, at least I had six days before I had to preach again, but it felt like just three.

A sign on the right side of the road caught my attention, a sign for a Sunday night blues jam at a local bar. The button on my radio is set to the blues channel, right next to the one for BBC news. My blues, my truck, my dog, sitting by a river with a rare cigar: my secret pleasures that always helped me find and calm my noisy core. People sometimes laugh at blues music, maybe because it cracks open our secret thoughts and exposes the backroom narratives of our lives.

I sure wanted to go into that blues bar on my way home from church — but could I? Could I actually enter that dark den that I had been shaped to be afraid of?

11

For three weeks I ignored that sign. But finally, one Sunday, I told Deb that I was gonna be out for the evening. I knew she had plenty to do, getting ready for the art classes she taught at a Christian high school. She said, "Great, need dinner?" I said no, I would have roots and sprouts and flax seeds for dinner (our code for McDonald's drive-through).

Why couldn't I tell my wife I was going to a blues bar? Not because she would have disapproved. I just didn't want to crack open my tired, angry, limping flow of thoughts.

Wardrobe selection: blend in with the crowd that would likely show up at a blues bar. Jeans, baseball cap, tee shirt — basic preacher camo.

After a nervous drive, I parked and walked into a dark room: spooky lighting, musicians up front, and about 30+ people in even darker seats. The smell of beer, leather, and liquor hit me right away. The range of folks sitting there hit me second: men and women, almost all ages, various shades of skin. But it was the fear of being outed — as a pastor! — that hit me hardest.

I sat in the back, feeling very out of place and surprisingly at home at the same time. The floor could barely be seen, and the table was sticky. The waitress called me "honey pie" and asked for my drink order. I said, tea with lemon. "Really, hon?"

This was not a great start, and I hoped for no more questions. I felt like an imposter, sitting with a group of people who warmly greeted one another with real and lingering hugs.

Dammit, for weeks afterward, that waitress had a pitcher of tea ready for me each time I walked in. Yes, I had become a Sunday regular. The place began to be familiar, with remnants of the Saturday night crowd lingering in the barroom (and especially in the bathroom. Oh, the bathroom. Do you wash your hands and use the paper towel to open the door? Me neither, ha, cough.) People ages 40 to 80 years occupied the seats and the stage, bikers and homeowners and yuppies and at least one preacher-in-hiding. Gandalf tells the Hobbits, "Not all who wander are lost" — a thought that seemed to apply well to my fellow-wanderers.

But how could *I* be a wanderer? I was living out my calling of building a church home. No longer would we be nomads, taking shifts in various school cafeterias. We had started a church 20 years ago, and finally, three years ago, we began worshipping in our own "built from scratch" church building. It was a gorgeous building and a great accomplishment, amazing that our young men and women could pull off such a feat. It was the building that mattered, right? You could touch it, walk inside, and feel that you had a *church home*.

But my church had a pastor who was, let's be honest, pretty terrible at administrative tasks. Often my feet felt like they were in cement that had not yet hardened; I could move them, but only with great determination. Who was in charge of what, anyway? Well, many of the responsibilities were mine. The mortgage became my nightmare. It had to be paid every month! Didn't the bankers understand that we were a *nonprofit church*, just trying to do good things?

Each Sunday, after the service, I stood at the door to the parking lot to shake the hands of my dear congregants. These were people who lived the blues — in their marriages, health crises, job demands. They dealt with insomnia and family struggles. This was where I felt God's pleasure, pastoring alongside people's hurts. But now that we had our building, I became stuck in daily conversations about the morning's offering, about typos in the church bulletin, about the thermostat setting, about who was assigned for nursery duty that morning. And whose job was *this*, whose job was *that*, *whose job was it*??

Something happened, the fourth week I went to my blues bar. The singer and the lead guitar player were singing a song by Stevie Ray Vaughn, *The Sky is Crying*.

Something happened in me. Something got cracked open and got exposed. The message, the word "baby," the singer feeling his music with his fingertips and words, something caught me by surprise. I felt like crying, and it had been a long time coming. I did it in a quiet, manlike, preacher-in-hiding kind of way. The waitress came over at that exact moment to ask if she could bring more tea, and dammit, she caught me.

Body language started speaking all around me. People were connecting with the singer — and not in a happy, "gonna party like it's 1999" kind of way. But quietly. There was a connection between the musicians and the audience of people, people who would probably never talk to each other in sunlight hours. I felt a rocking motion in the music, like an old lady with a new baby, like an autistic child seeking to find his center, like people who needed to cry but had nowhere to go, and no one to give them the space for their sorrows.

This is what a lot of blues music is about: how the weight of the human experience is just too much, sometimes. "My baby left me" seems to weave through most blues music. But "baby" could be my girlfriend, my wife, my health, my miscarried baby, my dead father who I never said "sorry" to, my waistline, my dog who got run over, ... Suffering and blues: the common ground for the biker, the yuppie, the waitress, and one hiding pastor. In the blues bar, "I'm sorry, man" is how the men spoke to one another, a hand on a shoulder. The women talked and sometimes cried with the other women. "Forsaken" is the cry; someone to listen is the hidden desire; and *being heard* is the start of redemption.

And people started dancing. I have to tell you that I love to dance; great memories of swing dancing in high school, at proms and in the one dance contest my girlfriend and I won because we could put the crazy in swing. And when I've traveled in Africa, over the last 24 years, I found that the all-out dancing was the key to connecting, later, during the interactive sermon.

But this dancing in the blues bar was different. It was adult, bluesy, a less-is-more kind of movement. The connection between partners was a kind of *moving conversation*. The musicians, the audience, and the dancers were all grooving to the same beat and the same message: "Yeah, my baby left me." It wasn't a drunken, bawdy, bragging, quick-pick-up kind of environment. It was a philosophy of life that we had all come to know and share, just a band of broken travelers. I began to discover a unique tribe called *blues people*. The music, the lyrics, and the company provided some kind of real comfort, like telling someone what hurts and the other person listens and believes you. For me, the pastor, this was a new kind of listening. And maybe that's what the haunting message really was: listen for when *your* hurt is spoken in a song.

In a confused way, I looked forward to my weekly blues adventure. When I left preaching each Sunday morning, the sign along the road was waiting there to remind me of my appointment later that night. Deb asked me about the blues bar and what it was like inside. I gave her vague answers, I don't know why. I guess I didn't want to admit I was excited about going there. Sunday morning was my calling, my official responsibility . . . and it wasn't much fun anymore. Sunday night had become my recreation, my freedom from responsibility.

It also became a fascinating laboratory where faith could meet real life. For years I had walked on Christian carpet, talked Christian talk to Christians, did Christian handshakes and drank Christian coffee. I had moved farther and farther away from the 83 percent of Americans who are not connected to a church family — drifted away from my first love, as the young, naive church "planter" who actually *believed* in evangelism. Maybe this wasn't Christian talk, but it spoke directly to me.

And more: this new adventure had the drumbeat of danger in the background, a thumping that was always in my ears in those days, that I would argue with or try to ignore. I knew I was in danger of losing the war to keep the church going. The mortgage was crushing, the numbers of people dwindling, the conflicts becoming more acrid. Often I just wanted to run away from it all. Was the blues bar really a mask for my failed struggle? Was I taking refuge in this somewhat pretentious pastime in order to make a "meaningful" exit from the church? I was afraid to connect those dots. Too much to lose.

I had been coming to the blues bar every week for four months, sitting in my self-assigned seat, breathing in the conversations around me, making gentle eye contact and doing a few fist bumps with some other people on this weekly blues cruise. I had in fact made the long journey from five tables back to three tables back from the stage. One evening, when the musicians were taking a break, one woman turned to me and asked a basic but frightening question. "What do you do?" she asked bluntly. Was this really happening? This was my refuge, I was off the clock. And the truth was, my baby was not doing very well. My hesitation was, um, awkward, drawing more attention.

The waitress happened to buzz by at that moment. "I think he's a priest," she announced. Dammit, where did that come from? Had I even spoken to these people? Well, of course I had. I am a preacher who talks to anyone, maybe not always so subtle about getting into a stranger's hidden story. My camo was clearly not working. But the group took the remark sarcastically.

"Did you hear the one about the priest who went into a blues bar?" I was preparing a jokey answer when another woman scrutinized my face and said, "You *are*, aren't you!" (By the way, a blues bar has only one word for a religious guy, a "priest.") The woman was watching me steadily. The waitress seemed delighted to have caught me sitting in my oh-so-blended duck blind, waiting for unsuspecting birds to land nearby. But when I looked around and saw their faces, I could see that the group was mortified, shading into anger. I felt their shame and hurt.

"Why are you here?" someone challenged me.

"Are we your project?" another said, with an edge of hostility. Even in panic I could visualize the news story: "Preacher gets butt kicked in local blues bar."

The group quieted when the musicians came back on. Things seemed to get back to normal — the new normal. Some people would not speak to me for several weeks, as if I was radioactive. You see, at the bar I had a ringside seat, a peek at the score: who's sleeping with who, who was behind on child support, who needed a place to stay, who was sick of their 6am to 8pm routine. And of course, all the crude jokes. People felt betrayed.

But I kept coming back. This was not just their refuge, it was mine too. But now something shifted. Each week, someone would ask me to *pray for them*. They wanted a

18

prayer for their children, or about the court case with the ex, or the unpaid taxes. Someone's child had been screaming on the phone, in hurt or in rage. The health issues brought a special desperation: motorcycle accidents, cancer, therapist appointments to pay for. And there were "white collar" prayer requests, about downsizing, resumes, attorney's fees.

I was a bit ashamed of my own attitude. I didn't want to be the pastor. I craved being one of the guys; I wanted emotional filling, not draining. This might be a new adventure, but I wasn't sure I wanted in. Selfishly, I wanted to be left alone. I felt an awkward tension, sitting in the supposed "den of sin" while feeling the pleasure — and the pressure — of God's work in and around me.

For my blues friends (as I thought of them) my presence created another kind of tension. They would pour out their confidences in a slow, "less is more" kind of tempo, in the hope that someone might possibly be listening. After all, their blues "priest" might have an in with the Guy upstairs. Hidden from view, of course, was the preacher who was also seeking the Guy upstairs.

By now, I was the semi-official blues bar preacher. Every week, it seemed, I would be called to the back of the bar to pray with someone who was crying. My presence would often trigger anger: "F____ God and F____ the church!" I was trespassing on their turf, no longer safely ensconced in an elevated pulpit. The anger went deep, going back decades and even farther back, into their own father's life story. Anger was often followed by tears that they thought had been hidden, under control. Strangely, I felt at home here, praying with them, listening to them, never showing shock or disgust at their blaspheming. And each week when I walked in I received lingering hugs and fist bumps from people I had come to know and love.

So, naturally, I asked the blues organizer if we could host a session at my church. "You nuts?" he said. "I'm serious," I assured him, "and we can *pay the musicians*." A blues player being paid was the magic wand. They came to the church on a Sunday afternoon, seemingly scared that they would be struck by lightning. It was too loud, and the group didn't seem to match the building. I wondered if some of the church folks would catch a glimpse of this crowd and make an appointment to come talk with me in my office.

When I came home I asked Deb if I could invite some friends over for a Christmas party. Deb said, "Okayyyy," wondering what was coming at her, what would happen in our front yard and to our reputation. I explained, "Some friends from the blues bar are looking for a Christmas party." Ok, I was stretching the truth. I just wanted to invite them over, maybe to make up for crashing their Sunday blues jam, maybe so I could be one of them, maybe because my church was going downhill. I didn't know why, but at least it would be a fun adventure.

And it was. Fifty people came to our not-so-big house. It was packed, sort of like a popular Friday night happy hour. I even found a Christmas blues "station" on Pandora to play in the background. These were not the church people I spoke to every Sunday morning. But I was beginning to feel at home with my new buds who were willing to give me a chance. Some of them seemed amazed that this "priest" actually lived in a house, had children and a wife and a dog. Some had a cautious look, almost not blinking in order to stay vigilant and not let the cuss words flow like DC traffic. I saw looks being exchanged, which I interpreted as, "When's the sermon coming?" "What's the catch?" and "I need a smoke, man."

I called for attention to offer a prayer, and everyone bowed their heads. I said thanks for the food, and for each soul in the room, and I asked for help and encouragement for each person at whatever struggle they faced, and then I gave thanks for Jesus at Christmas. When I said Amen, many others whispered "Amen" too.

I didn't know where this was all going. Something new was bubbling inside me — and it was about time, too. Back when Deb and I got married, we moved to Northern Virginia with our two passions, art (hers) and evangelism (mine). As with everyone, we soon got caught up in "doing life": buying a house, fixing it often; managing cars and attending plays and our kids' soccer practices. All wonderful things that make life worth waking up for. But at the same time, I had strayed from my passion. I had moved from evangelism to church maintenance. Deb was able to stay focused on her craft, developing art curriculum, taking art trips to NYC and Europe, earning her masters at the Corcoran Gallery.

And now, where was *I*? I was now pastoring a group of newcomers, people who were missing their old church. You see, their *old* church had a great youth group, a hired nursery worker, and a Ph.D. pastor who was their close buddy. But I still loved pastoring people at their need places. I still had building goals. And I focused constantly on giving the unchurched a way into the church building. The unchurched wouldn't come.

Right after Christmas, Deb and I threw a Super Bowl party for my blues bar buddies. This time, 60 people showed up, a little more relaxed now, a little more trusting. Some brought their children. The blues bar waitress had become an avid gatherer of people. "Oh, you better be at Pastor Al's house *or else*, and yes, I'm talkin' to *you*!" It was again a sweet time — light on religion, but with a simple prayer for God's blessings and presence. Three people separately asked me for prayers.

But my actual church was still struggling, more and more. Finally a dear, longtime friend, one of the church elders, said the unthinkable: "We need to sell this building." It zapped me like the shock I got as a child, when I put my finger in a Christmas tree light socket on a dare. But this was even less fun. Seven acres, 13,000 square feet. Stained glass windows and vaulted ceilings. We had worked so hard for it, sweat and worry and prayers, and then the victory celebrations. All for naught. This was something bigger than I could process. I went to the blues bar and I started to rock, trying to find my center, as the singer launched into the great B.B. King song, *Nobody loves me but my mother.*

Several weeks passed. The waitress asked me about Easter service. Oh right, the crowning day of the Christian faith! But I was too exhausted to find any passion. By now I had preached over 25 Easter sermons, all lost somewhere in my office files. I mumbled that all would be welcome at our church and please come, said in a pastor's recorded voice. Soon enough, word came back: pretty much *nobody* would come to the church. There were lots of jokes — that lightning would strike them, about needing larger glasses for communion, about fear of being converted. And there were other, whispered comments: they want your money; churches are like sales booths, once you go in you can't get out. "Why would I go there to learn to be a hypocrite when I'm *already* one?"

It all brought back my own wounded memories of being in church as a child. A pastor saying "I told you so" at a time of crisis. Getting funny looks because of my clothes or my haircut, or not knowing the protocol. The shame around divorces, fear of hellfire and brimstone, and feeling unable to measure up to the God people's standards. What could I say to reassure my new friends, who all had their own wounded memories? One dear soul, the best smoker and drinker in the place, summed it all up. She put her arm around my neck and slurred, "Al, I already know I'm a loser, so I don't need to go to your church to hear that from you."

Their community was the people around them in the blues bar, people who were honest about their pain and troubles — not the church. Each week the blues faithful would come in, hug one another for real, and buy each other a few rounds. Then they would sit for a few hours, quietly murmuring "yep" to the lyrics of hardship a-coming again.

Then the waitress (dammit) spoke up again as she bounced by, "Hey, you could have your service here!"

"Right," I thought. Let's hold Easter service in a dirty, vomit-from-Saturday-night place where people would mock God and make their jokes about faith. What would I tell Deb? Even though I often find the jokes funny, sometimes my defenses kick in. Don't people understand there's a line that shouldn't be crossed? Don't they know that I need to defend God's name? The truth is, God can handle Himself just fine. God can handle the mysterious tension of fake mockery and real mocking, while hunting for a soul's salvation all the time. This God, I realized, *could feel right at home in a blues bar.*

I had a dear friend in the bar who I'll call Diane, a lawyer in her day job. Diane was the person who could talk to the owner about getting the place ready. So asked her about this idea, and she immediately responded. "Are you freakin' crazy?"

The next morning, I was sitting in my other bar (Starbucks) when my phone rang. Diane asked me, "Al, did you do some freakin' voodoo thing to me?" "Sure," I said, "tell me which spell it was that worked on you?" Yes, Diane was up for organizing the Easter service. And she did it. She got the bar fixed up, hired a cleaner, gathered Easter crafts for the children, found a bunch of musicians, put banners up with crosses throughout the bar, and brought in 20 bundles of flowers to decorate the tables and the

24

permanently sticky bar. She even organized a potluck lunch to follow the service, setting up plywood tops and tablecloths on the pool tables and sending out invitations. She worked like a dog.

On Easter Sunday, 55 people came in, with mixed fear and delight showing on their faces. Someone asked, "Are we really doing Easter here? Can this be a good thing, Pastor Al?" I had graduated from "Priest" to "Al" and now to Pastor Al, which was okay too.

People came all dressed up, some in collared shirts and simple dresses, some dressed fancier for church. I sensed a fear in the room about what I would say. Would it be about hell fire and brimstone, the old bait and switch trick? Would I make them feel guilty? Would I maybe call for a *decision* right in front of their friends? I noticed the lingering hugs and the whispers. I prayed I would stay on mission, a mission still in its discovery phase.

I preached my sermon on, "What resurrection are you counting on?" Is it about finding your soulmate? Getting your kids to turn out right? Finding the perfect job? Getting your health all fixed? I then made a case for Jesus, who died for sinners like Pastor Al and rose again, and is preparing a place for me and you.

In the midst of speaking the message, I felt what I can only describe as God's pleasure. It felt as if I was loving *with* God, in that moment with my new buddies. I had preached that morning in the church building, to the regular church folks, but the afternoon was for the blues group. Both were very real, both had precious people present, both had the resurrection story. But the blues group somehow made me feel God's pleasure.

When I finished speaking, one of the musicians, a bass player, began to sing "Amazing Grace," in his gravelly, broken-by-life voice. He sang as if he desperately needed *that* song, that morning. The whole room shifted, from fearful to a softened soul. Something had shifted in me as well, and forever. This was a kind of evangelism that brought with it some new thoughts and habits and a transformation of my soul. Were these people my buddies first and foremost, and "targets" for evangelism sometime later?

The clear truth is that we have found a commitment to one another. On a recent Sunday, the bar owner had a question for me. She was excited about the plans for our Christmas service and party, and she asked if everyone could bring cookies. I suddenly realized that this was not a church that met in a blues bar; we were a blues bar that also met for church.

All my life people have told me I was a good listener, but the truth is, I usually listened *to reply*. I was trained to reply. In fact, Western Christianity is built on "having an answer and giving a reply." Having a reply proved my spirituality, my pastoral credentials, and my intellect — right? But this dark and gritty little blues bar had taught me something else. It taught me *listening to hear*. I would sit there and listen for my own hurt to be spoken, in the blues lyrics sung on stage. The people at the blues bar were all, like me, hearing their own thoughts, sorrows, and grievances in the blues lyrics. We were enough alike that we also heard each other in the sound of the blues.

This new adventure of mine was not in Africa or somewhere in the Pacific. I had found comfort — even found a home — as a missionary to an unreached group near my own church. I had to learn, and I'm learning, their customs, taboos, and hang-ups, while I am still learning about my own.

What adventure awaits you in the pages ahead? If I promised you an amazing revolution of your soul, you would think, "Sure — another promise waiting to be broken." If I told you that this is the silver bullet for evangelism, you would find another book to download. What I can tell you is this: Something has changed for evangelism, something that is mega big. The Judeo-Christian Ethic is a museum exhibit. Uncertainty and cynicism rule; people are not entering the church buildings any more.

I believe that the core truths of the Christian faith are as real and true today as they ever were. But we have lost our stride with evangelism, trying to share our faith. We think we know where the unchurched think, hunt, hide, and shop. Dance teachers talk about "dancing in the wild," which just means taking what you learned in the dance studio and trying it out on the dance floor of some restaurant or bar on a Friday night. The teachers know that many students will not venture beyond the safety of the ballroom studio and into the blues bar. These chapters are based on my experiences in the wild. They have brought me to love even more the studio — that is, the church world — and my hope is that you might also have your own cherished adventures in the wild.

Chapter 2

It's All about Suffering (Not Just Apologetics)

Speakin with my mouth, sure I know the way
But my heart won't follow my words, no way.
My heart looks around, asks me . . . are you OK?
So my mouth gets louder, *I know the way.*
But my heart can't follow, my words betray.
My heart's chasing my words and my words betray.

— Al Dayhoff, *My heart is chasing me*

I was hiding in my blues bar, listening to Albert King's *Born Under a Bad Sign.* I could hear in its mournful words the haunting moan of the original curse of humanity. Albert King got it. He felt it, he traveled with it in his nightmares, and maybe he lived it. The tortured, booming blues sound retold the story of Adam, of all of us, locked out of Paradise. I try to imagine that angel, who was created to protect and bless Adam, gripping the sword to be used on God's first-created human, if he didn't vacate the premises! The same story many of my blues people experience, through court judgments and restraining orders.

We don't know much about Albert King's early life. His father was a priest, who left the family of 13 children when Albert King was five years old. Pretty much all we know is what he captured in his perilous sounds, the lyrics too-close-for-comfort, the sweaty blues performances. He, too, was no doubt a traveler who could tell his own story of being locked out of paradise, of the times when the soul can't suppress its rage: *"What's wrong with this world?"*

I *get* that journey. I've been on it my whole life, and maybe you have too. My parents rose from their brokenness, but still, to some degree, they passed it on to me — the feeling of being a misfit in a world full of glossy advertisements, beckoning to a shiny new brand of life. Often as I preached from the pulpit about God's forgiveness and free Grace, I was in a personal tailspin about my position in God's universe.

How I got here

My pain has a history; it starts with a pivotal moment. A man named Murray Gillespie stood alone one evening, balancing his weight on a bridge in Baltimore, Maryland. The smoke-blackened bridge spanned a railroad track that once defined Baltimore's working-class ethos. Baltimore was familiar with the clangingly loud sounds of people hammering, hauling, and welding things. This was maybe 1955. Dwight D. Eisenhower was still president. The first official advisors were sent to Vietnam, and Ray Kroc opened his first McDonald's in Des Plaines, Illinois. Hurricane Diane hit the northeast United States, killing 200 people and causing over $1 billion in damage. Rosa Parks was arrested for refusing to give up her seat on a bus to a white person, and the national civil rights movement began. That same year, Murray Gillespie jumped from his bridge into the path of the unstoppable train; he died with no one present.

Murray Gillespie was my grandfather. Alcoholism, adultery, unemployment, separation from his children, and the wounds of his own childhood had pressed down on his soul. No pastor, no apologetic was there to reason with him and shift his decision. I suppose his last thought might have been, "Just get this endless suffering cycle *over with*." I heard this story as a child, and over the years I have imagined, hundreds of times, his body hitting the front of a speeding train.

Murray was born in 1920 in Quebec, Canada — one of seven children born to Annie Gillespie. Annie was married to a sea captain, who often came home drunk and in a rage. The family could only find so many places to hide from his anger. Annie was known for her cooking, and the one safe place for the seven children was her love-made food. One night the captain came home in a drunken rage, threw a lighted lantern and burned down the family home. Annie lived to bury all seven of her children, who died one by one, from alcohol addiction and its consequences.

Murray Gillespie left two children, Hope and Murray Jr. He named his daughter after a grandmother he loved, Hope Atwood, and by the time she was 12 (the year he died), he had written her three letters. Hope is my mother.

The spiral of anger, alcohol, drugs, pornography, and an endless list of addictions formed a kind of loop in the movie of our family, always playing in a new theatre. As a child, Hope was shuffled around Baltimore between wherever her grandmother was living and her mother's raging, "yell-all-night" home that offered few safe places to hide. She was often in charge of her four half brothers and sisters; it wasn't pretty. When Hope was 13, one of the "rich" boys invited Hope to a party at his house. I should mention that Hope had one bold, shocking gift: she was gorgeous, though she didn't know it. Men would gawk, employers would open a path, and a jealous mother would try to sabotage her.

Well, Hope got pregnant by the rich boy, and his father offered her $500 to make the abortion happen. Hope didn't know what "abortion" meant, and when the doctor told her, she refused. The doctor promised Hope that she would be given the address of the foster parents' home, after the birth. But after the baby — my older brother — was born, Hope went into a coma for nine days. She was too weak to see the baby for three months, but she finally found the baby and took him home.

Things went from bad to hell bad. At the age of 15, Hope left her mother's home, invested a quarter in a newspaper, found an apartment, lied about her age, and showed up for a job interview at the Stiff Silver Company. Her photos as a young woman resemble the pictures of Lucille Ball from the 1920s; the gift of beauty helped to open doors, which always mystified her. She was soon put in charge of leading busloads of tourists around the factory and explaining how each department worked. Her job responsibilities grew, and before long she was making $42 a week — an amount that, for a 15-year-old who had lied about her age represented unknown security, a dreamscape experience. She had a single driving motive: to get a home of her own and get her baby back full time.

Then a man moved into the room across the hall from her tiny apartment. He was a foreigner, clearly older than she was, and clearly interested. Hope avoided him, always hurrying in and out of her door. Her experience was that men die or they abuse you, or both. The man persisted, knocking on her door to ask her out. Unable to fend him off, she simply moved out the first time he went on a trip. She wrote him a note: "Please don't look for me," explaining that he was too old for her. It took him three months to find her, and he pursued her until she finally relented and agreed to marry him.

What was he like? Did he treat her well? Did she secretly like him? Or was she just too worn down to refuse him? The wedding was attended only by the pastor and his wife. The groom brought the marriage certificate; it showed his age as 36 years old, divorced, and Hope's age at 16. Hope protested that she was only 15, but she signed the paper. She was by now in a full anxiety attack, and the groom actually said her vows for her.

That man was my father, also named Al; I was born shortly thereafter.

Hope still wrestled with a life that gave her so few options and little space for self-expression, while her marriage got tougher. That film loop of her grandfather's and her parents' stories seemed destined to make its ugly return. Hope's marriage started out as the same story: constant fighting, late nights and lost time, adultery and addictions

— until something unexpected arrived in the mail. It was a tract from the Oliver B. Greene ministry that explained *how to become a Christian*. Hope prayed the prayer, and a new journey began, one with its own bumps and landmines.

By the time she was 22, Hope had five children with Al. But now, with her new faith, she had started a new family story. The five little lives had moved her, urged her, to find meaning for those children, something that she had never known. And she managed to bring my father along on her journey.

My dad, so much older than mom, died in 2010 at the good old age of 87. Dad had become the rock in the ever-present storm, someone who would seek peace in whatever room he entered. I especially remember the delight in my father's eyes when I made something in carpentry or a construction project, or placed in a gymnastics or wrestling competition. I remember eyes that were always approving, with a sense that he, too, was being honored as my father. I miss him terribly.

Pain lifts the veil

I often hear people complain, talking about church people, about the "happy, happy, happy" image we project. C.S. Lewis put his finger on the answer: *"Pain removes the veil; it plants the flag of truth."* I have told you my history so that you can fully understand my pain, which I no longer try to hide. We honestly do not need to channel those singing Doublemint twins from the 1970s commercials, who banished their troubles with chewing gum as they frolicked, never blinking, in the sunshine. How often have

I tried to "sell" Jesus with a happy jingle, suppressing my own blues tune — fearful that my own sorrows and demons might expose my weaknesses and undermine the sales pitch?

But the unchurched are not buying the happy pitch; it doesn't square with the bad-luck life they are living. My blues buddies were seasoned life travelers and they didn't mind telling me off: "F*** the church" and "f*** your GOD-D***** Christianity!" Or they ask, in many ways and states of mind, "Where was your God, when my child was taken from me?"

One day, Lester stopped into the blues bar for the first time. When he heard the waitress call me Pastor Al — I had given up trying to stop her — he turned and challenged me: why the f*** was I in a blues bar anyway? He quickly apologized for his "French" — but he was seriously upset. "My God-d***** wife left me tonight, threw all my clothes in the dumpster and took our car. And to top off my evening I have to sit next to you! F*** this, I'm gone! Oh, and God bless you, *Pastor Al*." Lester had no emotional space for an unwanted encounter; all his reserves had been used up by his pain. The kind of pain that makes an animal caught in a trap chew its own leg off to find freedom — freedom without a leg.

I did not grow up in a Doublemint commercial, and neither did many or most of the Christians I know. My dad's suicide was only two thoughts away, and there was discord in all the relationships around me. I remember the year when I was preaching a series of sermons on making

35

a "Biblical Marriage" — in a season when Deb and I were not in a good place ourselves. Deb served in the Sunday school that year, just so I wouldn't have to meet her eyes in the sanctuary as I offered my message of uplift. Evangelism offers a little more cover: it's most often one or two conversations with a stranger, never threatening the crooked places in my soul. But speaking in church on Sunday to the parishioners who come every week presents a challenge, if you have a few truths you'd prefer to hide. So, we perfect a kind of a dualism, a contrast between the life we really live and the life we present in our "witnessing monologues." We aren't telling the whole truth, and perhaps our motives are even hidden from ourselves. Perhaps we need to hide from our own stories. The real, unstoppable human storyline is *loss*.

Loss is in fact our oldest storyline, with its roots back in Genesis 3:

> Cursed is the ground because of you;
>> through painful toil you will eat food from it
>> all the days of your life.
> It will produce thorns and thistles for you,
>> and you will eat the plants of the field.
> By the sweat of your brow
>> you will eat your food
> until you return to the ground,
>> since from it you were taken;
> for dust you are
>> and to dust you will return.

It's not the answers that drive us to God — it's the *hurts*. It's our aching questions that show us His eyes and His arms open to us, and His Son suffering on the cross. The soul feels all the hurt of our great fall and is driven to seek God: and this is pain's purpose. Only God can awaken the soul from struggle and distress.

Seminary students, for over a century, have been trained in the power of apologetics, studying the many reasons for turning to God. Apologetics surely have value — but might this be a smaller piece of the puzzle than we think? The apologetics writings of Lee Strobel, Josh McDowell, Ravi Zacharias, Norman L. Geisler, and Timothy Keller are inspiring works, to read again and again. Non-Christian scholars are similarly inspired by the miraculous design of the natural world. But these arguments relating to facts and figures will never be enough to change the heart.

Maybe the church has been immersed for too long in the debates of the last century, studiously responding to Nietzsche's famous claim that "God is dead" ("Is God Dead?" *Time Magazine*, Apr. 8, 1966). With the discoveries of modern science, it was argued, there was now no need for faith or religion to explain the physical world. God's sphere became too small to fit in people's daily lives. The church answered Nietzsche's challenge with volumes of proofs and alarmist diatribes — and doubled down on apologetics classes for Master of Divinity students.

But it's not working. About 18 percent of the population claims to be part of a church, even if that means attending only once a month, or twice a year. Some predict that the number will drop to 14 percent by the year 2020. Today, the Christian story has been lost for so many. In 1966, the words "In God We Trust," imprinted on our money, had meaning. Faith in God was a cornerstone of Western thought, lived in courthouses and schoolrooms and discussed around many dinner tables. Today, we live in a very different place. The Judeo-Christian ethic has given way to an age of fear, turbulence, and cynicism. The apologetics scholar, too, amid all the research and writing, feels suffering in the soul. The United States counts nearly 40,000 suicides a year, as well as an untold number of attempts. In my 25 years as a pastor, I have learned that the burdens and ways of the soul are cryptic and deep; the soul may hold its secrets even at death. But whatever the reasons for suicide, it is clear that many harbor untold suffering.

That is why I propose that the turnstile of evangelism, today, must pivot not on apologetics but on human suffering. Of course, scholars have not disregarded suffering in studying the soul's track to God. But now, the soul's crisis needs to take center stage. The world today seems to be crying out, "If your God is so great, *why is my life so damn bad?*" But the secret hope is buried somewhere, the hope that it's all true — that we can meet our creator somehow. The big questions cycle in our souls every day. "Where did I come from?" "What am I doing here?" "What happens after death?" And our suffering seems to point us away from faith in God: "This God does not like me much because my life is so tough. Why does He assign this homework of suffering?"

One evening in the blues bar, after I had been outed as a pastor, one man challenged me — not to give him answers, but to *listen*. "If you all would just shut the hell up," he said, "maybe you could hear what we have to say about our lives." I answered, "Tell me more." He then shared with me his own long cycle of suffering, admitting that he had never told anyone this before. I was glad to see him, later, at the Easter service we held in the blues bar.

There he would hear another great, true story about suffering. In Luke 23, Jesus suffers more than any human being ever will. But he speaks to the crucified thief who is without hope, lost in his pain. Then the saved thief begs him, "Jesus, *remember me*, when you come into your kingdom." Jesus answers, "Truly, I tell you, today you will be with me in paradise." Remember me: the message of the blues.

We all have the opportunity to share, at the point where the promise of eternity, bought by Christ on the Cross, breaks the temporal time loop. There is hope for us, that we can have eternity itself set alongside our real temporal suffering. These promises are sometimes not easy for any of us to believe. Perhaps the first step toward talking with the unchurched about pain and suffering is to admit that we ourselves have not fully come to terms with suffering either.

The island of misfits

Maybe it's time for us to consider the thinking of the unchurched. When we ask people for their candid responses about evangelism, we find something surprising: Both the speaker and the receiver tell us that the evangelism moment is not really transparent. To be transparent, as speakers we need to be completely honest. The outer person speaks to us, rejecting God and asking for proof, and we meet the challenge with our apologetics. Meanwhile, it is the person's inner soul that wrestles with the image of his Creator, pondering the universal human questions: "Where did I come from?" "Why am I here?" "Where do I go after death?" Evangelists must listen well in order to hear these deeper questions. And we must listen even more carefully to the questions our own soul is asking. Perhaps it is time for us to recognize that our pain is what makes us human, and to become more transparent in our suffering. We are all seeking our Creator, and we are all broken.

Let me tell you the story of "Rudolph the Red-Nosed Reindeer," a Christmas special that was first aired on Sunday, December 6, 1964. It has been telecast every year since then, making it the longest-running Christmas TV special in history. Rudolph is rejected by his peers and superiors because his nose is cosmic bright. So Rudolph runs away with two other "misfit" friends (a great setting for a blues lyric!). They stumble across "The Island of Misfit Toys," where unwanted playthings languish until the island's ruler, King Moonracer (a winged lion), can find homes for them. The King agrees to let the three runaways stay for one night, in exchange for a promise from Rudolph: as soon as he returns to the North Pole, he will ask Santa Claus to deliver the Misfit Toys to children. After cliff-hanging adventures, Rudolph's shining nose becomes a critical savior in a terrible blizzard: when Santa cannot manage to deliver his toys, Rudolph agrees to go, if he can also pick up the unwanted Misfit Toys to deliver to children.

We know the feeling of being unwanted, lost on an island with no way home. But we are lost together. And a winged lion is fighting on our side. Our suffering isn't wasted: it is God's mysterious tool that is used to help the world, at the end of the story.

In the blues bar one Sunday night, a man in his sixties came and sat near me. He looked a little stiff and out of place; maybe he wanted to be in hiding for a few hours. In church, of course, I would walk around and greet people, and I was expected to do so, but here in the bar, leaving people alone was expected. So I let him be. A bit later, when someone I knew came in, he introduced us, and then he whispered to me: "Steve lost both his wife and daughter to cancer two months ago." Thunderstruck, I began to cry quietly. I was glad it was dark.

> The Lord is near to the brokenhearted and saves the crushed in spirit. — *Psalm 34:18*

Chapter 3

We Are Not Present

I can see your body, you're right there,
But do your thoughts have care.
I see your body, hear your breath, know you're here,
and I'm asking if your thoughts have care.
I can see your body, but I see you're not here.
I always wonder if your thoughts have care.

— Al Dayhoff, *I can see your body*

Thank God for those moms who organize those father-daughter dances, the ones who make centerpieces all glitter and sprinkles, who dim the room just right for self-conscious "couples," who set out the little paper plates and matching cups. They know how to create a space for that awkward, "OMG" dance — encouraging men who, in their day job, might be writing top-secret code for a military satellite, to actually dance and mingle.

Each year from first grade to eighth, my friend Jeff and I would huddle in a corner, make fun of each other, and then go out on the floor and dance with our daughters. They, of course, were beaming with little girl beauty: a beauty we wished, in our old dad hearts, would never, never change. Coming into this setting was like waking up in a bowl of Jello — everything looked strange. But if I could, I would like to thank those ladies who gave me a whole file of treasured memories with my daughter.

Erin and I went to our dad and daughter dances for seven years. Each year she would start talking about outfits three months ahead. It took me a lot longer to realize that I needed to contemplate clothing. I was familiar with a variety of clothes: I had a bright orange outfit for when I went deer hunting; I would outfit my duffle bag with a floppy hat (along with a venom extraction kit) before going on a mission trip to Africa. Unfortunately, these outfits would not work for this occasion. I finally asked Erin for help. Who could have known that my "outfit" should in some way match her outfit? Fathers are like Captain America: we will rise to defeat any evil that could cause our little girl even a moment of fear — even fear of a fashion disaster. But Erin rescued us both. She picked out my black suit and black shoes, plus a tie that matched the color of her dress.

Erin and I rode together in my old truck to the dance. In the passenger's seat next to me was one of the two precious children I was given in this life. Now eight years old, wearing a flower brooch on her dress, she was battling with the seat belt and trying to get settled. In little girls, God brought beauty into the world, and sitting here next to me was God doing His best art. So, why was my mind so far away, embroiled in its own conflict? This was one of those times I was trying not to pray for someone I truly hated. I was thinking about all his faults and offenses, picturing myself winning our epic debate, seeing this difficult person punished for the wrongs he did. Even as a pastor, is any of us immune to anger, jealousy, and even

44

deep hatred? I have to admit that a black, dungeon-like moment was brewing inside of me.

Then, breaking in as if from far away, I heard Erin's voice challenging me. "Dad. Dad, you there? DAD? DAD?!! Where are you?" I had completely lost awareness of where I was, and who I was with. I had lost sight of this rare moment. Captain America was driving the truck but totally oblivious, despite his fancy shield and matching socks. At one of the most precious moments my short life on earth could offer, I had gone missing. I had fallen into a dungeon and couldn't get myself out.

For me, this was a bellwether moment, when I realized I had traded something so big for something so trivial. Even ten years later, my mind often drifts to this teaching moment. How many of us, in our lonely old age, might pine silently over the lost opportunity to take our little girl to a dance?

At other moments, too, we are not always present with the people God has brought into our lives. Some of these are people that He wants us to share our faith with, and we miss the opportunity to truly connect with them. For me, the question arises: If we are not present in those moments of evangelism, where are we?

Driving to the dance, I was present in my anger instead of with my daughter. As busy 21st-century people, there are many places our minds can travel to. But I suspect we may be in our pain, in our own fear, or even in our theology and our scripts, instead of in the gospel.

We are in our pain

I was a brand new driver, 17 years old. I saw the car in front of me swerve to the left, lurch as if it hit a speed bump, swerve back to the right, and speed off. Few cars were around on this country road. It was dark and hard to see, so I stopped in the middle of the road. Something was lying in the road, something scary, something out of a horror movie. I wanted to just drive off and not look at what was there in the road; I still wish I had. Someone's dog was lying in the road, half-crushed from the speeding car, on its way to a terrible, slow death.

Ours was an animal-loving family; we had goldfish and 1500-pound steers and everything in between. I would say that I lived in a zoo and really meant, I lived in a zoo. My mother was a living, breathing Dr. Doolittle! She could talk to the animals, and they would say something back. (Don't ask me to prove this, because I will change the subject.) I walked over to see if I could help that dying dog.

The large dog had a collar, which meant an owner — someone who cared for him. When I tried to comfort the dog, he snapped like a harpooned alligator, barely missing me. But the pain had used up all the cells in his half-alive body. Now I heard someone. A middle-aged couple was walking out from the lawn nearby. It was their dog, and I was the person with the car at the scene of this horrific moment. I'm beginning to cry as I write this, remembering the woman's cry, the saddest noise I had ever heard. I stood there as the person who had hit their dog, still writhing in sickening pain. After a minute the man

46

dragged his sobbing wife away; she was hitting him. Another neighbor showed up with a gun and quickly shot the dog in the head. Silence. He looked at me and said, "You can go son; things happen."

I never actually told them it wasn't me. I didn't want to bring everyone more pain, and I was just hoping to forget. But that's not how our mind behaves, of course. I went to my math class the next morning, and I couldn't focus. The numbers were blurred on the page. In woodshop (my favorite class) I couldn't focus either. I skipped lunch. Later that day I threw up, overwhelmed by the horror of what I had seen.

Just as the dog's whole being was consumed with physical pain, our minds can also be consumed with pain, sometimes physical, and sometimes other kinds. Our minds are consumed with conflicts we haven't laid to rest: conflicts between family members, job difficulties, our children's struggles with learning disabilities or other problems, a crazy health scare or a bad medical report, and all our other grim realities. We are not present, when our lives and minds are filled with the decibels of noisy souls.

What uses up all the space where "being present" needs to be nurtured? Our pain does. Pain can use up all our extra space and push out the opportunity to grow a new relationship. Our minds continue to grind over our past marriages, the mental illness of a parent, loss of money (whether due to gambling or bad decisions or dumb luck), the disrespect that comes with being not smart enough or big enough or thin enough or pretty enough—on and on.

You know, the touch of the Savior's hands and words came to so many people who were in pain. The woman at the well; the blind man; the thief hanging on the cross. Their pain wasn't always resolved, but His presence made the pain bearable, even meaningful. He can turn down the volume of the noisy, hurting soul. As a child I can remember screaming like I was dying when I scraped my knee, but once Mom was there, the pain mattered less. Her knowing and caring got me back in motion, ready for my next skinned knee.

Once, when I was traveling in Florida, I was privileged to provide this caring presence. I was sitting in a chair near the beach, and a very attractive couple came and sat nearby. She was a beautiful Indian woman, wearing a—well—a bathing suit that only an Indian Beauty Princess was authorized to wear. The man was someone I could only describe as the Hulk, like the comic book character but without the green hue. His muscles had muscles, and then some. So here I am, sitting in a force field of beauty and strength that could not be charted. I've learned to appreciate God's humor, and I wondered if some divine appointment was possibly unfolding. I truly hoped not. Looking at her would do something to me, and looking at him could end my life fast.

Anxiously aware of this powerful man beside me, unexpected words came out of my mouth: "Dude I'm not even looking at her."

He laughed and said, "No problem man."

This was good, now I was free to sit quietly and keep to myself. Then he asked, "Where are you from?"

"Virginia," I answered. He was quiet for some time, and then said, "My dad was from Virginia."

"Does he still live there?"

"No; he died last year."

"I'm sorry, my friend."

The hulk started to cry, and I said, "Tell me more." He recounted how his father had been such a jackass his whole life, and he had just died, at 57 years old.

"I never told him goodbye, I'm sorry for being such an idiot [he used more colorful words], and I never told him I loved him."

The Indian princess stopped putting on lotion and took off her sunglasses.

I'm not sure why, but the words that came out of my mouth were: "I sense God feels your pain and cries too."

The hulk gave me this look, like a child who needs to cry, but can't. And then he just put his hand on my shoulder and sobbed. The Indian princess became a statue. He said, "Are you a religious guy or something?" I said I was a Christian working my way through life as God showed me the way. Then came the words. "You know, I hate it when people give me advice I don't ask for; you're the first religious guy to not tell me what to do and then just repeat it every time I see them." His wife then invited me to an Indian dinner at their home, next time I was in town.

God had given me a gift, in allowing an authentic, free-flowing work of the Holy Spirit to take place with that Indian princess and the broken Hulk.

We are in our fears

At five, I remember fearing the impending arrival of my younger brother or sister. Where would it sleep? Whose food would it eat? How long would it stay in our house? Later, at seven, I was worried sick that I couldn't be Spiderman at Halloween. The Spiderman outfit lay waiting in a box under the steps, but in our house, it was first-come first-served to the costume box. At 12 years old I feared I would stay short forever: wrestling in the 98-pound weight class in 8th grade, I was a real chick magnet (not!). At 16 my fears were a bit more serious. I feared having no escape from my parents' home, that I would live there till I was 17! Unthinkable!

As an adult, fear unfortunately did not go away. My Hebrew teacher in seminary struck fear into me like no one ever had. I often thought, "I could take this guy with one hand tied around my ankle" — but that never helped my grade. More than anything else, I feared hearing him say, "Mr. Dayhoff will be reading for us today." It was like living in the movie Dumb and Dumber.

That was before fear really arrived in my life. I became a father. Wesley bounced into our lives when Deb and I were in our late 20s. I worried constantly; every night I would go into his room to see if he was breathing. I had read all the advice about putting kids on their backs or their stomachs (or maybe letting them free range in the backyard?). I couldn't sleep till I saw his little chest moving. Knowing Wesley, I imagine he would have held his breath on purpose if he thought I was watching. The fear plagued my thoughts and kept me from sleep.

Fears follow every age in life. They grow with us, like moles on our skin. Similar fears stalk all of us and rule over us in our weak moments. Fear has had sway in my own lifespace, far too much. And it keeps us from being present, because fear, like a self-absorbed child, demands to be the center of attention. But the Lord never intended us to live in fear, and the scriptures teach us that fear cripples the soul. 1 John 4:8 reads, "There is no fear in love. But perfect love drives out fear, because fear has to do with punishment. The one who fears is not made perfect in love."

I remember the time I saw a bird fly through an open door and into our home, when I was about 10 years old. A 10-year-old boy watches with mischievous delight as a free-for-all unfolds at such rare wonderful moments. My mom was deathly afraid of birds flying in the house. Add two little sisters, and you've got a scene like the running of the bulls in Spain. I sat in sheer happiness appreciating how a little bird could herd and terrify everyone, creating chaos, a spastic flying around of legs and arms. You couldn't pay for this kind of entertainment! But to those terrified, fear controls and steals with devilish precision. To hear our Savior's voice and feel His touch begins with understanding our weakness. It is not in our own strength that we swat the fears away — His love does the work for us. Love does for us what we cannot do for ourselves.

We are in our theology

I recently went to a blues festival in Wheeling, WV. It was a delightful setting, the performers' stage set off by the backdrop of the Ohio River. I listened to blues while watching people fish. Such simple joy, baby! But in front of the stage stood the inevitable security guys, big mean men in squishing t-shirts who would delight in a little brawl if anyone tried to touch the musicians. Such were the Pharisees in their teaching and ways.

The Pharisees loved the best seats in the synagogues because it gave them positional authority (though not the personal connection people crave with their faith leaders). Jesus was at that time being studied by pilgrims who had come from all over Israel to participate in the Passover feast. One of the first things Jesus said to the people was to be cautious of the way of the Scribe and Pharisee. (Cf. Mark 12:38-40; Luke 20:45-47.) He observed that they were seated "in Moses' seat." These leaders were not the real thing, but merely usurpers of God's anointing and power. Still, their position had to be recognized, as guardians of the law. Jesus instructed, "All therefore whatsoever they bid you observe, that observe and do" (23:3). Jesus then pointed out their hypocrisy: "But do not go after their works: for they say, and do not" (v. 3). The Pharisees laid heavy burdens on the lives of the people, but offered no help to make those burdens lighter. They acted as though they lived such holy lives that the burdens of the average person, like getting shingles or a bounced check, never happened to them. Jesus was not telling people to follow the self-serving teachings of the Pharisees, but to follow the teachings that rose from the Law of Moses.

The Scribes were associated with the Pharisees, and their job included the transmission of religious texts and other legal and historical documents. But their religious labors were done to impress men, to create a separation between "the righteous and unrighteous man," rather than to grow closer to God. They wore the Scriptures bound to their forehead and to their left wrist. Jesus said they did this to create a barrier and to be seen by other men, instead of being present in people's lives. They enlarged the borders of their garments and then their tassels, which were visible signs that they were holy men to be respected and obeyed. Jesus, in His instruction, reminded them that they had forgotten the preeminence of the real and anointed God, the Messiah, the heart of their journey and life in God.

Like the Pharisees and Scribes, when I usurp God's glory, I muster my cunning side. It's in the tone, in using complex words rarely spoken by ordinary people, that I assert my pride. My well-articulated theological beliefs can serve as a buffer between me and the people around me. I enjoy and feel safe in the delusional position of being "more right" than others in my life.

Perhaps we are prone to find ourselves in our theology, rather than in the presence of the human beings God has placed in our lives. Too many churchgoers have drifted into a church attendance that has become habit; we do it because we have always done it.

In my journey of seeking the unchurched person's perspective, I often hear people cite the "religion routine" they inherited from their parents, as the underpinning of their belief system.

I think of my friend, "Ben." His parents got divorced early in life, and the inevitable question came: "What should we do with this child our failed marriage made?" The divorce was so painful, and the child such a reminder of the disastrous union, that they decided to send him away to boarding school. It was a prestigious "solution" to a "mistake" that arose from intimacy. Ben spent his life reciting the theological underpinnings given to him by his parents. Yet, it was very clear to me that he simply wanted his parents' presence in his ordinary life journey. He always made them proud, with grades and athletic accomplishments, and then his deep, introspective gaze would sometimes tear away the curtain to reveal the real narrative. He wanted them to be present.

Ben's family was a family of faith. Their story, I think, speaks to a disturbing trend among Christians. Many have been marginalized and depersonalized by a mentor who was strong in their life theology (maybe a father, mother, sibling, or teacher) — and they pass on that same marginalizing attitude in their network of God-given relationships. How many of us have drifted into observing the mechanics of our faith, without experiencing its energy, its presence in God's shocking creation? Do we miss the wonders of a loving God who is busy preparing a place for us for when our labors here on earth are over? As God delighted in walking in the Garden of Eden with Adam, he was feeding the relationship with His very presence. Theology is meant to create a presence, not shield us from the intimate contact of being with other people.

We are in our scripts

I am the first believer that God can use anything, anytime, anywhere, to instigate faith and salvation, in any soul. God is the ultimate artist, in my mind, and I'm seeing daily how He paints. Can God use a child's spontaneous observations to call a mom to faith? Sure. Can God use the sunset, in all its beauty from the window of a New York skyscraper, to redeem a blind man? Yep. Can God use the hallucinogenic high of a cocaine user to see, feel, and argue himself to faith? Uh huh. God can use the most pathetic and poorly-formed gospel proposals, and He can choose not to anoint the clearest gospel speech ever heard. It's God that provides the power to save and awaken a soul.

Having said all that, I come from the era of Christian Scripts. Thank God for them! They are well-intentioned and at times very effective. The Roman Road, The 4 Laws, the Bridge Illustration, the EE question — "If God were to say, 'Why should I let you into my heaven?' what would you say?" Please hear that I fully believe all of these are helpful to instigate and teach the gospel in people's hearts. However, I think something has changed. A growing population is doubtful about the scripts and procedures we use. People are longing for something more authentic.

It's when we get a question that we haven't been trained to answer that the cracks begin to show. People are onto the "pitch," the recording, a trained approach, a script. One person in my blues bar network turned to me and said, "Oh I've heard that a million times, that's all you got?"

But we have to say something, right? We have to use words in a certain order or logic, to tell the gospel?

Matthew 16:13–20 gives us an exchange of Jesus with the disciples:

13 When Jesus came to the region of Caesarea Philippi, he asked his disciples, "Who do people say the Son of Man is?"
14 They replied, "Some say John the Baptist; others say Elijah; and still others, Jeremiah or one of the prophets."
15 "But what about you?" he asked. "Who do you say I am?"
16 Simon Peter answered, "You are the Messiah, the Son of the living God."

What is interesting is that, up to this point, Jesus allowed long spaces of time to flow by without ever instructing the disciples on who He was. The key moment came when Jesus turned to the disciples and asked, "Who do you say that I am?" It took a long time of being present with the disciples to lead up to the acid question.

Scripts can be useful and we know that generations benefited from them. Yes, we do need to get the information out about how to receive Jesus and come to faith. But I wonder what would happen if we ourselves were truly present in more of our evangelism interactions.

At one of my evangelism seminars, I asked the people around the table, "What do you fear about evangelism?" The answers they gave were stunningly honest. They feared conflict and rejection. They were afraid they were lying, that they were creating confusion, that they would fail. And they were afraid that someone would discover the mess in their own lives and families. How do we find a way to accept our own fears and failings, so we can be more present with the people we are talking with?

Being present

Marina Abramovic is a Serbian-born, New York-based performance artist who describes herself as "the grandmother of performance art." Her art explores the relationship between performer and audience, the limits of the body, and how communication can happen or be prevented. From March 14 to May 31, 2010, the Museum of Modern Art in NYC held a major presentation of Abramovic's work—the biggest exhibition of performance art in MoMA's history. During the run of the exhibition, Abramovic performed "The Artist is Present" — a 736-hour static, silent piece, in which she sat immobile in the museum's atrium, while spectators were invited to take turns sitting opposite her. The program broke attendance records, attracting more than 850,000 visitors.

During the exhibit, some people came and stood in line 10 times to sit with her; one man sat with her looking into her eyes for seven hours. Person after person after person stood in line for hours to experience a still, silent connection with Marina, in the sterile setting of a museum with hundreds looking on. People described a spiritual experience, something they have never had, but longed for. Maybe it was the need to be seen, or the need for a space where the unspoken communication could be heard, as if loud and articulate. Maybe many craved the attention of someone who would simply be quiet and be with them, even as hundreds looked on. How did so many people manage to be "alone with Marina" in that setting? Being present with someone, having a core that is quiet and at rest, has its own loudness. This begins to define the spiritual encounter with God.

There are videos of Marina Abramovic on YouTube that show clearly the simple but profound skill of being present with someone. Many begin to cry after just a few minutes — maybe because, for the first time, they feel valuable enough to have another person look at them, directly and deeply, examining the story in their eyes and exhibiting no fear, in this human encounter that is slow, unfolding, and full of unscripted surprises.

The exhibition had such a deep impact on the participants that a support group for the "sitters," *Sitting with Marina*, was established on Facebook, complete with its own blog. Questions swirled around this art presentation: What was it? Why did so many people come again and again? How could one person sitting in silence with another have such dramatic impact on so many people? Sitting silent, how hard could that be? As hard as raising the titanic out of frigid water, apparently. The people who sat opposite Marina described the experience as life-changing, the unzipping of the soul, being seen by someone, finally connecting with another human being. Marina's knowledge of how to be present had been forged by a life of struggle, pain, and denial, of being invisible to key people in her life. What she had been denied, she learned to give to others, and she made it an art form.

Is this similar to what God did with Adam as he walked in the garden, enjoying his company and presence? Perhaps there is a side of us that communicates without words or scripts or proposals, feeding the starving souls of others in our lives. Perhaps it's about perceiving that the other person wants to be with you and isn't in a rush to get away from you. I believe much of Western evangelism is rooted in the notion of a stranger walking up to a stranger, actions that appear strange in our current culture. Marina demonstrated a simple, rare and life-changing moment, being present with someone.

We are not present. We are not present in the lives and minds of the people God has brought into our lives. The hidden truth is that this is a silent, devious cancer within the faith relationships that God has enabled us to pursue.

> It is better to go to a house of mourning
> Than to go to a house of feasting,
> Because that is the end of every man,
> And the living takes it to heart.

Sorrow is better than laughter,
For when a face is sad a heart may be happy.

Ecclesiastes 7:2-3

Chapter 4

Where He's Sent Us

Got a life full of time, where should I go?
Got a wallet full of money,
A head full of ideas,
Got a God-given mission,
And I need to know, where should I go?

Got a story full of people,
Got all my struggles,
Experience I can't explain,
Got to turn and look at where I've been.
Got a God full of mission,
I'll know where to go when I know where I've been.

— Al Dayhoff, *Where should I go?*

Suppose that Gladys Love Smith had not met Vernon Presley in 1933, at the Evangelical First Assembly of God Church in East Tupelo. Why would that matter? Well, there would have been no Elvis Presley. When their eyes met at church, and a little ordinary, awkward conversation started between two young people, who could have imagined that a multi-billion-dollar industry would be the result? Elvis Presley has sold (it is estimated) more than one billion record units worldwide, more than anyone other singer in record industry history. Elvis had 149 songs appear on Billboard's "Hot 100 Pop Chart" in America.

But there is another side to the story. Few know or remember about Jesse Garon Presley, Elvis's still-born twin brother. How did the baby's death affect Gladys, Vernon, and Elvis? When he was growing up, Elvis heard a mysterious voice that he believed was his brother Jesse. Not much is known about how Elvis revisited the memory of his lost twin, nor how his parents grieved or contemplated Jesse's growing up years that never happened. But families everywhere can't stop asking "what if," about those taken too young. The story behind the story of Elvis Presley's life is fascinating, heart-breaking, and full of hidden secrets — maybe hidden from Elvis himself.

Like it or not, your family is a central piece of the person you are now. I had a vivid reminder of this one day, walking toward a public bathroom. Just in front of me was an elderly World War II vet, beginning to struggle with the door handle. As I leaned forward to open the door for him I seemed to enter into his space — a comfortable space, furnished with the familiar buttoned plaid shirts and Old Spice aftershave that always reminded me of my own father. So, once we were inside and I saw him lose his balance while standing at the urinal, it was just second nature to reach out to steady him, and I held onto him until he had finished his errand. Then he turned to me and said simply, "Thank you, soldier." No matter how long I live, I know that the WWII generation will stay in my memory: after all, God sent me to a soldier.

All families are great messy stories, waiting for some narrative to organize all the people, events, and experiences unique to our personal history. Family storytelling is so important to the next generation and the next. Genesis 45 is one of the greatest messy family stories in all of the Bible, telling the story of Joseph in embarrassing detail. It's the story of someone realizing where he had been sent in the past so that lives would be saved in the future. Family chaos, stolen dignity, mysterious meetings, and a rags-to-riches story worthy of a PBS special. Let's take a look.

Did God send Joseph into Egypt?

Joseph was the son of Jacob and his beloved wife, Rachel. Because he loved Rachel so much, Jacob showed partiality towards Joseph, fashioning for him a "coat of many colors" — an act that elevated his position and infuriated Jacob's other sons (by his other wives). Family jealousy ran rampant. Matters worsened when Joseph started having dreams. He dreamed that his brothers' sheaves of wheat bowed to his, and he had the poor judgment to share this dream with his siblings. His second dream compounded their resentment, with the sun and moon (symbolizing his dad and mom) also bowing before him.

One day, amid this tension, Jacob sent Joseph out to check on his brothers, working in the fields. The brothers, consumed with anger, looked for a way to get rid of him. Reuben, as the eldest, was responsible for the safety of his younger brothers, and he balked at the idea of killing Joseph outright. As a compromise, he suggested that they throw him into a deep well. Some Midianite merchantmen happened by, and the decision to sell Joseph rather than let him die in the cistern spared his life but sealed his fate. The brothers then bloodied Joseph's pretty coat and agreed to tell Jacob that a wild animal had eaten him.

Having been sold into slavery, Joseph was eventually bought by Potiphar, the captain of Pharaoh's guard. "And the Lord was with Joseph" (Gen. 39:2). In no time at all, Joseph proved his mettle, and Potiphar made him an overseer in his house. Potiphar delegated everything to Joseph except for the preparation of the food for Potiphar himself. However, Joseph's position was complicated by Potiphar's wife, who tried day after day to persuade Joseph to "lie with her." Joseph repeatedly refused, out of respect for both Potiphar and God. Finally, Potiphar's wife lost patience and grabbed him. He fled, losing his garment, which she kept as evidence, and accused Joseph of trying to rape her, reminding Potiphar that he was the one who had "brought this slave" into their house.

Potiphar could have had Joseph killed on the spot. Instead, he had Joseph thrown into prison. "And the Lord was with Joseph" (Gen. 39:21). Soon enough, Joseph was an overseer of the other prisoners: when Pharaoh's cupbearer and his baker were thrown into prison, Joseph was assigned to them. When they both had disturbing dreams, Joseph was empowered by God to interpret their meaning. His interpretations were correct: the baker was hanged, and the cupbearer was released from prison and restored to his previous position.

Two years had passed, when Pharaoh had a troubling dream that no one could help him interpret. It was then that the cupbearer remembered Joseph's skilled interpretations. He was sent for, and he told Pharaoh the meaning of the dream: seven years of plenty would be followed by seven years of famine in the land of Egypt. Out of gratitude, Pharaoh hired Joseph on the spot, giving him his signet ring (as a symbol of his authority), as well as a new name and an Egyptian wife, Asenath. Joseph's job was to store up grain for the famine to come. After seven years, the famine indeed hit, and Joseph served as the administrator of the grain stores he had prepared.

While Joseph was distributing grain in Egypt, Jacob and his sons were suffering from famine in Canaan. They had no grain. Jacob sent his sons to beg for grain from Pharaoh's stores. The brothers were brought before Joseph, who recognized them, though they did not recognize him. As they bowed before him, Joseph remembered his first dreams, when their sheaves of wheat bowed before his. He spoke harshly, accusing them of coming to spy out the weakness of the kingdom, and finally offered to test them. One of them could go back home to fetch their youngest brother — who was Joseph's full brother, Benjamin. The others would remain confined in Egypt.

Jacob refused to let his beloved Benjamin go to Egypt. But the famine continued. Finally, the day came when they had no grain. Eventually Jacob realized there were no other options. He was distraught, but had to agree to send Benjamin, laden with gifts for the "man in Egypt." When his brothers arrived, Joseph invited them all to dine with him. The brothers were fearful of some kind of trick, but Joseph's steward reassured them that God was behind it all

(Gen 43:23). They feasted — but separately, as it was forbidden for Egyptians to eat with Hebrews. When the brothers prepared to depart, they were laden with sacks of grain, and all the money they had paid was also returned to them, concealed in their sacks without their knowledge. And Joseph had his steward hide his own silver goblet in Benjamin's sack.

The brothers left bright and early in the morning. Shortly afterwards, Joseph told his steward to go after them. The brothers swore they had done nothing wrong. The bags were searched, and the goblet was found in Benjamin's bag. They returned to Egypt to beg for mercy, and their lives. Joseph offered to let them go — if Benjamin remained behind as his slave. This time, the brothers did the right thing. Judah pleaded for the life of Benjamin, telling Joseph their father would die if they left Benjamin behind. He offered himself for the freedom of Benjamin.

This righteous act was too much for Joseph. He sent all the Egyptians away so he could make himself known to his brothers. He forgave their sending him to Egypt, saying God meant it for good, and they exchanged many hugs and kisses. The brothers returned bringing the amazing news to Jacob, who could hardly wait to pack up and go see his long-lost son. Jacob, with 66 wives and descendants, moved to Egypt. After he met Joseph, the elderly father said, "Now I can die" (Gen. 46:30).

Genesis 45 speaks a timeless truth awaiting our embrace. Listen to Joseph's clarity about the events of his life. Do you hear bitterness or the need for revenge? Is he crying over the lost years, or confused about the meaning of all the threads? Listen again:

> Then Joseph said to his brothers, "Come close to me." When they had done so, he said, "I am your brother Joseph, the one you sold into Egypt! And now, do not be distressed and do not be angry with yourselves for selling me here, because it was to save lives that God sent me ahead of you. For two years now there has been famine in the land, and for the next five years there will be no plowing and reaping. But God sent me ahead of you to preserve for you a remnant on earth and to save your lives by a great deliverance. So then, *it was not you who sent me here, but God*. He made me father to Pharaoh, lord of his entire household and ruler of all Egypt."

Joseph's story was epic, for sure. But when we flip through the stories of so many lives — including yours and mine — we begin to realize that *all* our lives have an epic storyline. The Christian community does well at looking at the past and teaching how God saves sinners. We use language like "God plucked me out" or "lifted me," or "saved me from my past ways." But our full, unvarnished histories are even more valuable, as they tell of the preparation and investment God puts into our future labors. The seeds of our future callings are often encased in these past experiences.

You see, we can't have clarity about where God is sending us to save lives until we come to terms with our own storyline, with all of the situations, feelings, and faces we can remember. A memory bank can bring up the past for us in a nanosecond, when we hear a song, smell a certain food cooking, or shiver from cold wind. The past is so full of God touches and shaping, things that do not easily fit into a "God plucked me out" testimony. So, maybe we choose to forget. But God overrides our forgetting efforts with a story that rises and falls at His will, as He sends us into the future to save lives.

We have done a good job thinking and preaching about being saved from our own pasts. But we don't know where God is sending us until we know where God has sent us. So, our own messy family story holds a mother lode of clues for how, where, why, and when God is gonna move with meaning, in and through our seemingly ordinary lives. Joseph, speaking with newfound clarity, declares: "It was God who designed this trail of events that led me right to where I am right now."

Why did God have Moses born to a servant, sent down the Nile River, and raised in a king's palace? Why did God keep David in solitude with his sheep, way back in the hills, for years and years? Why was Hosea put through a rough and unfair marriage to Gomer? Time and space are God's servants, to prepare His children to live redemptive, potent, evangelistic lives.

God sent me to a soldier

My father was a World War II vet who shipped on the USS Prairie. He was always young-looking for his age, but he was significantly older than my friends' dads. So, when I see an old World War II vet wearing a funny hat with strange words and numbers on it, maybe in a parade or just sitting on a bench, mustering all the dignity he deserves in his old feeble age, I feel right at home walking up to him and saying, "Thank you for your service, sir." To me, they are never strange aliens in funny old clothes with mean grimaces. They are my father. God sent me this father; I did not choose him. And as this World War II generation has almost died out, the question of where these veterans will spend eternity is on my mind — because God sent me to a soldier.

A few years ago, I was doing an evangelism seminar in the Northeast. A wonderful group of Christians gathered, mostly professionals in their 50s and 60s. They had been in the church for most of their lives. I have an exercise I go through with the participants, to revisit the stories of their lives. The challenge is always to provide a safe setting for people to do the hard work of remembering their unique stories — events long forgotten, people lost in the back of their minds, experiences suppressed and hidden on purpose by the soul seeking to guard his host. I asked the group to take the next 25 minutes and write down "the story of your life."

At the end of the allotted time, I began by asking, "Can someone tell me the story of before you were born?" One man answered, "My grandmother was a Christian who always had hymns playing in her home." The next said, "I was baptized when I was eight days old." A little disappointed at their safe, sanitized answers, I then asked about the first five years of life. One lady said she remembered her Sunday school teacher, and the church dress her mom always dressed her in. Another spoke about singing "Happy Birthday" to Jesus on Christmas morning.

I was beginning to feel annoyed — and I know I don't hide it well (even though I've practiced in front of a mirror). So I said, "I need to apologize to you; I think I've set you up." I wanted to deflect the annoyance onto myself, as the group looked at me with growing distrust. Now I took a chance and just dove into what I hoped was the deep end of the pool. I turned to the lady to my right, made eye contact, and said, "Can you tell me about the *real* story of your life?" There was silence for a long awkward moment, and then some tears. And then harder tears, and she said, "I will not." Idiot that I am, I couldn't leave it alone, so I ventured right in where smarter fools fear to go. My eyes held hers as I asked, "Why?" She burst out in anger and hurt, "My husband was an elder in this church and he recently divorced me." Wow. Now I have to worry about the poor pastor sitting in with the group. Have I wrecked his church, or only set up a barrage of phone calls to his office on Monday morning?

Then something special happened. This dear lady turned out to be the kindling needed to start the fire going. Out came a procession of cancers, divorces, drunken fathers or grandfathers; the runaway children, the years of silence between siblings, the stories of people dying too soon and too young. There were the cries of the orphan, the stories of special needs children, the secret desire to play the saxophone, the lyrics of lost unfindable love, like an Elvis Presley song.

I always give the following instruction in these seminars: "If a crime or wrongful sexual act was committed against you, you might just use the code, 'for your eyes only.'" So, later that day, I saw sheets with the code written: "For your eyes only." After the session, a number of people came up to me and said, "Thank you, Al." Lost memories had been found, and events that were too big to digest all at once had put them on a new course of remembering and honoring their life stories. One that might take days or years to evaluate.

We in the Christian community may have a "tone problem," though probably not intentional. We may have a bit of a superiority complex, as we communicate the raw data of our faith and how it squares with life's key questions. How do we shift tone, from a "king talking to a peasant" to "one beggar asking another beggar for bread"? The bridge is there: it is the *real* story of our lives. Is our redemption proposal worth anything, if it can't be applied to our own lives first? We need the Christian world to tell the pain-strewn, ongoing story of where God has sent us — without any nice, clean conclusions. You see, the Christian is a beggar too, only we have forgotten our story. In the Christian community, we have perhaps gotten disconnected from our own stories because we feel that we have been *saved,* called out of our pasts never to return, because the way forward is full of light and new opportunity.

But we don't know where we are being sent until we know where God has sent us already. Where has God sent you? Can you remember? Is there a theology or character muscle that has prevented you from going back, way back, back to your grandparents, back to the stories that were hidden or hushed up at family gatherings? To a single mom, a racecar family, a Down's syndrome child, a bankruptcy, or lonely, prison-like toil in a factory? God sent Elvis a still-born brother, and He has sent the events in your life as well.

Evangelism begins to glow and blink like Rudolph's reindeer nose when we realize God sent us somewhere on purpose. God has built tracks in your past, crosstie by crosstie, rail by rail, spike by spike, so that you could ride into the future as a redemptive force. God is training and equipping to prepare you for his great work in the lives of other Christians, and in particular, in the lives of the unchurched, to help them hear their own stories. Because the non-Christian doesn't know where God has been, until they can recognize that He has been part of their crazy, awkward story all along.

> When my spirit was overwhelmed within me,
> Thou didst know my path.
>
> Psalm 142:3

Chapter 5

The Mother of All Questions

Hear my hurt! I show you the secret of my soul,
And you just give back your words about truth.
Hearing is two ways or it's no way.
One day your truth will stay home,
the day you want me to hear your hurt,
the secret of your soul.

— Al Dayhoff, *Hear my hurt*

Growing up, I was one of five siblings — three boys and two girls. The three brothers lived in the basement. I bunked with my younger brother Jeff; Bob, being three years older and the firstborn, got a room to himself. Bob was secure in himself. Being a great tennis player and leader of the pack in family order suited him well, and he rose well to the responsibility. When his chosen position as grand marshal of our family circus became tiring, he could always retreat into his solitary bedroom hideaway.

Late evening or early morning — well, actually, any damn moment of opportunity that presented itself — there would be espionage-like raids between mine and Bob's bedrooms. (My little brother, Jeff, had a blood pact with Bob, so an enviable peace held between them.) For some reason, Bob loved reptiles (despite the minute size of their brains), and he happened to have a strange, fear-inspiring guest living in his room. It was a four-foot iguana that he had raised from an eight-inch mail-order creature. I am not making this up. He would feed the beast a head of lettuce or, if money got tight, dog food as a substitute. The dogs never knew. Perhaps I was jealous of this stupid reptile that seemed to have such a nice bedroom to himself, with an endless supply of food and an owner who caught him large bugs for breakfast. (I was never jealous of the bugs.)

One of the stealth night raids I made on Bob's room was to reconfigure all the volume control knobs on the soundboard of his stereo system. (Yes, Bob had a stereo system as well as a large record collection, the kind that first-borns save for, organize, and file neatly.) So the plan was hatched, the sun's position in the sky was noted, and potential witnesses were observed to be busy with other things. I made my way into Bob's room — oh, the delight of all the little levers and knobs! I laughed as I changed them, thinking, grinch-like, of the sound that would result.

What happened next was something I had never imagined, in my ten-year-old reptilian brain. You see, Bob had placed his beloved iguana as an armored security guard, draped over the stereo in his room. I had only seen that stupid lizard in statue-like poses, and even wondered in the back of my mind if he was really alive or newly stuffed. But the iguana was fully alive now, and he did what iguanas are born to do: wind up and whip the enemy with their tails, which make up over half their body length. His tail hit me on the neck and continued around my neck and down the front of my chest. Oh, the sting of death! I couldn't yell or cry, let alone accuse anyone or even devise a plot to kill the iguana. His brain won the battle that day.

And then I heard my mother's voice: "Din-ner!" When she called, you came right away. As five hungry children knew, when food was served, a quick arrival to the table was expected. I grabbed a turtleneck from my drawer and put it on before I ran to dinner. I knew that, right after the dinner prayer, Mom's CT-scan vision would check over each child to detect any injuries, weapons, unusual smirks, or guilty, suspicious stillnesses. That laser beam would scan the four other kids in one minute and would then settle on me for three-plus hours. To be honest, I earned that laser-beam stare with stories I would rather not put in this book at this time. I always sat next to my father, whose right arm could kill me, and he liked it that way. Mom asked the mother question: "Allan, why are you wearing a turtleneck?" It was midsummer and of course sweltering. Mother's guilt was always the best ploy, so I said there were no clean clothes in my drawers. Whew — that hit had been only 30% effective, but a second hit was always possible. Across the table, my brother Bob began to look at me closely. This wasn't going to end well.

Mom said, "Al, look at Allan's neck under the turtleneck." I didn't dare stop Dad's probe with those WWII machinist's hands.

"Oh my goodness boy, where did you get that welt?" Dad kept pulling at my shirt, exposing the entire length of the lash around my neck and down my chest. It was raised a good quarter-inch off my skin. My brother Bob's eyebrows were now shooting to the sky, and a smile was spreading across his firstborn, long-awaiting-God's-justice face. I answered in a quiet monotone, "I ran into a branch in the woods." The answer seemed to take the heat off, as everyone knew that the woods was my first home and my bed my second. Mom asked if it hurt, and I said, "Not much." And for my brother, well, life was good and getting gooder. My lie might have diverted the parents' suspicion, but he knew better. He won that round, with a firstborn's discipline. We had tapioca pudding for dessert that night, but I passed on it, under the knowing look of Bob's well-deserved V-day celebration. The welt lasted for three months.

I had been sure that the turtleneck would hide the evidence of my crime, even from the CT scan of a loving, engaged mother. But a mother can't stop trying to keep her son safe; it's not an option. And I knew that my parents would be engaged. They never took refuge in the mantra, "He made his bed, let him lie in it." Instead they probed, they asked questions, and they grew to know the way to the emergency room by muscle memory.

Discovering us where we hide is one of the greatest things a parent can do for their child. God's care for us, too, is loud and evident, as He patiently watches us hide, calls our name, and waits for our answer. He wants to find us again and again, even when we think we're hiding so well from Him. In one of the greatest scenes in scripture, our proud father, our heavenly Father, describes our own birth and creation, almost like an awestruck young dad gazing through the nursery window at his firstborn. This is a picture of God's love replicated over and over, throughout His wondrous plan. Listen for the values and legacy God gives His children in Genesis 1:

Then God said, "Let us make mankind in our image, in our likeness, so that they may rule over the fish in the sea and the birds in the sky, over the livestock and all the wild animals, and over all the creatures that move along the ground." So God created mankind in his own image, in the image of God he created them; male and female he created them.

What do these words mean? They mean God created two thinking, creating, celebrating, introspective, self-checking beings, who would above all else have the ability to communicate with their Creator and hear His voice. God made man a *conscious* being, something that has always fascinated scholars in every stripe of schooling. The number of books, lectures, and graduate degrees focused on our state of being conscious is simply eye-popping. God has endowed all human beings with a shocking and alive inner thought world. In the garden, He delighted in walking, communing, and simply being present with His creation.

Then something happened. Evil arrived in God's created paradise. A plan was hatched, the position of the sun was noted, and the first espionage activity in the course of human history played out in Genesis 3:

Now, the serpent was more crafty than any of the wild animals the Lord God had made. He said to the woman, "Did God really say, 'You must not eat from any tree in the garden'?"

The woman said to the serpent, "We may eat fruit from the trees in the garden, but God did say, 'You must not eat fruit from the tree that is in the middle of the garden, and you must not touch it, or you will die.'"

"You will not certainly die," the serpent said to the woman. "For God knows that when you eat from it, your eyes will be opened, and you will be like God, knowing good and evil."

The scriptures tell a sad story about how the angel Lucifer sought to become God, fell away from God, and was now applying his broken craft to mankind — the brand new children in whom God delighted.

Adam and Eve of course took the bait. Pondering the rewards, they made an informed decision that would affect all of mankind. Lured by the serpent with the music of becoming God, they took the fruit from the tree and ate it, just as God had forbidden them to do. The "gotcha" moment is the saddest moment of all time. When the serpent won the battle, he no doubt wound up and whipped his tail, lashing Adam's neck, around the back and down the front of his chest. Adam and Eve's choice couldn't be taken back — they couldn't yell for help or claim the rights of a victim. The welt would last as long as the time of man to walk the earth. Then, something broke into the desperate moment: the voice of the parent spoke. Genesis 3 describes the immediate results of Adam and Eve's sin:

> Then the eyes of both of them were opened, and they realized they were naked; so they sewed fig leaves together and made coverings for themselves. Then the man and his wife heard the sound of the Lord God as he was walking in the garden in the cool of the day,

and they hid from the Lord God among the trees of the garden. But the Lord God called to the man, "Where are you?"

He answered, "I heard you in the garden, and I was afraid because I was naked; so I hid."

If I was directing this movie, God would surely have spoken away all the sheltering trees, leaving Adam and Eve bare in His presence, and He would do what the gods of the movies do — shout in anger, exuding rage and balls of fire. However, God does not do this; he does not even say, "I told you so." Instead, he begins with a question, perhaps the mother of all questions: *"Where are you?"* It was a question that recognized Adam's endowed ability to answer. It was a question that offered him dignity, the ability to answer and to hear his own words.

Have you ever seen a two-year-old hide? Or, for that matter, a ten-year-old hiding a serpent welt under a turtleneck in the presence of his mother? Both are easy to detect, hiding in plain sight. I was a bit distressed, as a new parent, when my little son Wes would play hide and seek (his favorite game) and actually think he was *hiding*, as I could see 93% of his body behind the table leg. His little two-year-old voice would yell, "You can't find me!!" — as I'm wondering, what gene pool did this child inherit? Would this be a condition that would last into his teens, would he ever pass the SAT exams and get into college?

Adam and Eve were hiding too, and God, of course, knew just where they were. He asked the question simply in order to talk with Adam! He valued the relationship and wanted an honest dialogue, wanted to hear His very image speak back. To a new reader of Genesis 3, it's a surprise that Adam offers a response to God. (The movie I would write probably wouldn't allow the guilty to speak.)

Adam spoke honestly and said he was afraid; something traumatic had happened to the world in which he was living. He also answered honestly that he was naked. One can only imagine the meaning of such a phrase, as nakedness lays open the physical body, of course, but also the conscience, the many rooms in the soul.

God, after speaking the mother of all questions, listened to Adam's fears, answers, and justification. And then he unleashed the weight and cancer of the Fall: *Cursed is the ground because of you; through painful toil you will eat food from it all the days of your life.*

The soul needs to tell the story of the Fall, and its weight upon its own fragile life. When I would sit in the blues bar and start a conversation with a person near me, I would programmatically ask "How are you?" And without fail would come out — what hurts.

You can often hear someone burst out and say, "What is wrong with this world?" — whenever wars or gruesome crimes are reported, or maybe a hurricane has wreaked havoc. The soul is speaking from the surface of the image of God, insisting that these things should not be so. Or the soul speaks out from its own torments, when it is seeking a sex change, or something to end its life, or drugs, alcohol, a fourth divorce. The soul is crying out, "Something is wrong here!" Even day to day, on our cell phones, in our jobs and marriages, we echo the ancient question of the soul: "Where am I?" I believe that the unchurched souls all around us are asking this question, throwing out less-than-satisfying answers and hiding behind bushes, fig leaves, turtlenecks. I believe many are secretly pondering this question all the time.

But when we talk to people, we often address them with little awareness of the questions swirling within them. We assume that the human mind is simple, like the reptilian brain, caught up in finding the next meal or job, a girl or a smart phone app. But perhaps there is far more going on there. Could it be that, just as God speaks the mother of all questions in the scripture, *all* humans carry this question around in their souls? Could it be that the soul wrestles, ponders, imagines, and hopes far more than we think is possible, as each of us asks, "*Where am I?*"

Sonny Boy Williamson sings the blues song, "One Way Out," describing a pair of lovers who are about to get caught by her husband as they hide in the bedroom. The apartment has only one way out — so the only solution is to risk climbing out the window, vowing never to let it happen again. It's the story of Adam, hearing God's footsteps and trying to hide. Maybe it's our brokenness that we can't seem to fix. Maybe we are hearing the voice of death itself. Suddenly we ask ourselves, "Where am I?" and we vow to never get caught this way again. We find ourselves hiding in that awkward spot again and again, until we finally turn and meet the man coming up the stairs. That great story in the scriptures encourages us to admit we are the man who is hiding, who is climbing out of the window, and the one who is coming to find us is God Himself, asking where we are.

Chapter 6

The Birth Line

I always hoped the steps I took
Would lead me towards you
Now I understand
That you arrived on time
By angles and degrees only when the day was right

— Emily Morrison, *I Bless the Day We Met*

When I came out of my layman "camouflage," and my friends all knew my line of work, I could always count on Tracy to deliver a shot across the bow any time I walked into the blues bar. Tracy was amused and delighted that I had ventured out of my religious closet into her world of bikers, blues, and beer. She could be mean when she wanted to, and I wondered when I would be on the receiving end of it, but mostly it was just ribbing. She would say things like, "You're not going to convert me today!" or, "Is Jim Bakker still in jail for stealing all that money from those little old ladies?" She wanted me to know that all of the tricks Christians play on the unsuspecting were well within her radar. These weekly run-ins with me were a kind of hobby; they never reached the point where I would stop coming, or wished she would go away. She would wait for me to walk in the bar. She would walk all the way across the room, touch my shoulder, and post her "No Trespassing" sign on any words of mine that might pull her into the religious world.

She would cuss at me and then sort of apologize, always in jest. And of course, she would talk loud enough for everyone else to hear, because she knew she spoke for them too; she enjoyed her growing and appreciative audience.

Something was up with Tracy. Maybe my Spidey-sense was tingling, or maybe I just saw her as a challenge, someone to outlast or even outwit, maybe land a reply that would stop her mocking altogether. Yet Tracy was someone that inched into my mind each week; I began looking forward to her signals of strength and comfort in her non-belief — in God, the church, or Jim Bakker. Maybe there's another option here, I thought. Maybe Tracy was being brought alive by God Himself, not in a loud, hands-thrown-in-the-air, "Hallelujah, I've seen the Light" kind of way — but something much smaller, a tiny conception begun by God himself in her heart.

Is a baby conscious of itself at conception? No. Is everything already working at conception that will the baby physically viable? Again, no. But life has started, and it will grow and develop in a hidden place until the right time, when birth will take place. I began to imagine Tracy as a host to God's Holy Spirit making His mysterious way into her. Maybe a pregnancy was in motion in her soul. When Tracy would protest my presence or my words, my thought was, perhaps she protests too much. I'm happy to say that she is now a regular attendee in our blues church community. We talk often, and she even whispers prayer requests to me, and she still taunts me about not EVER becoming a convert!

Memphis Slim sings a song about a mean watchdog that is surprisingly friendly to a man who (we surmise) is actually having an affair with the speaker's wife. I think of that mean watchdog wagging his tail when I think of Tracy's inner watchdog beginning to let down his guard, waiting and wanting to hear a prayer that will mean something to her. This is how God begins to shift us from our unsustainable loves to His ever-present love. The lover that the soul is always craving is God Himself. When his Holy Spirit is working, the watchdog begins to be charmed. The conception of faith is already taking place in the hidden places of the heart, and this takes time.

My own spiritual pregnancy

When I was an infant, my 15-year-old mother stood in line at the Baltimore welfare office. Much later, in an unguarded moment, she shared with me the anger she always felt, placed in a strange world with strange stares, in a process that stole her dignity. Off in the corner was a black-and-white TV, fuzzy, but the only distraction available. It showed a Billy Graham crusade: yet another messenger telling her what was wrong with her. But then something sparked, and her watchdog started to wag his tail. She accepted the call to receive Jesus. Maybe she had done so before, but this time she felt something burn alive inside her. Dignity could be found in the act of asking Jesus into her life. What did she have to lose?

Mom's arms holding her babies had something to do with the unfolding of this story. We know that each soul must stand alone in God's presence and receive God's invitation, but those arms were holding me for a reason. She wanted so much more for her children, in her own broken kind of way.

God's Spirit came into her life boldly, but into my life quietly and almost secretly. Flash forward to when I was 10, and we got the news about my Dad. He had driven to work in his VW bug, like he did every morning. This morning, negotiated a curve as he always did, but in the blinding glare of the morning winter sun, he did not see the stopped car sitting on the curve. He hit that car going 65 mph. We were told that the broken bones were too many to count; the steering wheel smashed through his rib cage; his head went through the window. The little car was crumpled like an aluminum foil ball you would throw in the trash. I remember, at his hospital bedside, the doctor told us to say goodbye. Those words could not come to me, even though I probably tried. Instead, the prayer cut loose. "God, if You're real, save my dad!" He lived. I figure that my spiritual pregnancy was maybe in its ninth month.

The Birth Line

> But by the grace of God I am what I am, and His grace to me was not without effect. No, I worked harder than all of them — yet not I, but the grace of God that was with me.
>
> — 1 Corinthians 15: 10

Often when I think about my story, it is easy to forget all that personal history. Instead, I am tempted to credit my salvation to the sermon that immediately preceded my conversion to Christ. (Cornelius Plantinga writes something similar: "When I contemplate my own conversion experience, I am tempted to hang the time of enlightenment to God's truths upon the sermon of the preacher who immediately preceded the time when I committed my life to Christ.")

The pastor who gave that sermon has always been a bit of a hero in my mind, a large man who expressed large emotions as he talked about heaven and hell. At the end of his message, he issued a passionate invitation to anyone who would like to accept Jesus as personal Savior. I had not yet made the decision, and so, at the age of 13, I asked Jesus into my heart. But in reality, God was at work in my life long before that point. If my life were arranged along the Birth Line, it would show a long and careful journey towards Christ. A very real time of "pregnancy" took place, through the warp and woof of my life.

So far, we've been discussing the work of God to shape and influence us through life's experiences and encounters, and especially the mother of all questions, "Where are you?" But how do we come, personally, to put our trust in Jesus Christ? This is our Birth Line, our own faith journey.

This is not an easy topic to discuss. Where do we begin? Why do we suffer communication paralysis, when it comes to sharing our faith or conversion experience of becoming a Christian? I suspect that the message we give others doesn't really jibe with our own experience of becoming a Christian. We know that it took much more than a few minutes or hours, for Jesus to come into our own lives. It may be that the Christian community has paid too much attention to the moment of conversion and too little attention to the period of time that leads up to that moment.

Maybe we can start by asking ourselves this question: *"Where did I first experience the Lord's calling me to Himself?"* If we stop to take a closer look at our own process of coming to faith, we can bring that knowledge to bear upon our witness to others. It will revolutionize the way we minister, to respect God's schedule as it applies to other lives.

A resolution to this dilemma was first presented to me through the instruction of Reverend Steve Smallman, the former pastor of McLean Presbyterian Church in Virginia. Steve is a respected friend and mentor who has taught me a great deal about being a pastor and disciple. He introduced me to the concept of "the spiritual birth line." Steve suggests that, when Jesus talked about being born again (John 3:1-12), he intended for his audience to think about physical birth. Steve developed this diagram to illustrate the two "births" on one timeline.

Physical birth:
Conception – pregnancy – **Delivery** – Growth

Spiritual birth:
Life begins – Regeneration – **Conversion** –
   Sanctification

The physical birth line begins not at the time of visible birth, but rather at the time of conception. Similarly, the spiritual child is conceived well before the actual public event of profession! In fact, the spiritual birth line of the conversion experience begins, not with the moment of confessing Jesus as our Lord, but with the moment of physical conception, the implanted seed that leads up to physical birth and later to spiritual birth. Archibald Alexander likens this process to planting a seed: "The implantation of spiritual life in a soul dead in sin is an event the consequences of which will never end. When you plant an acorn, and it grows, you do not expect to see maturity; much less the ends of the majestic oak, which will expand its boughs and strike deeply into the earth its roots" (Alexander, p. 22). The true power of this birth line lies in helping us understand that God deals with us through a process of time, events, circumstances, people, and a multitude of other influences that all make piercing spiritual impressions upon our hearts and minds. Jesus understood that this process was occurring. In Scripture, we see again and again that Jesus attended to the current life needs of the people around him; he showed his awareness of the events that took place in their private lives. (Examples include Nicodemus, the woman at the well, and the calling of each of His disciples.)

Another illustration of the power of God making us "new people" is the picture of spiritual resurrection found in Ephesians 2. Verse 1 describes our condition when God met us: "As for you, you were dead in your transgressions and sins" — a deadness that only God can change. Verses 4 and 5 show the cause of spiritual conception: "But because of His great love for us, God who is rich in mercy, made us alive with Christ even when we were dead in transgressions; it is by grace you have been saved" (Ephesians 2:1 NIV). Verse 10 of Ephesians 1 shows the pregnancy period and the progress of the life principle of the Gospel: "For we are God's workmanship created in Christ Jesus to do good works, which God prepared in advance for us to do." The entire passage shows that when God plants the seed of faith in our hearts, it will eventually lead to the new birth.

As with the physical conception of a child, the time following that germination of life is filled with intimate nurturing moments and events. It is God who begins the process of spiritual life, and it is God who nurtures the seed of the Gospel, with many methods and messengers, until it comes time for that visible, tangible event: the time of the new birth! Jeremiah 31:3 reads, "The LORD appeared to us in the past, saying: "I have loved you with an everlasting love; I have drawn you with loving kindness."

While the power of God is indeed ready to regenerate the sinful hearts of mankind in a millisecond of time, His normal way of dealing with His children uses many molding influences. People are moved, drawn, and enlivened by God. You too, perhaps, were "chased down by the hound of heaven." But during the process of conversion, God's movement is sometimes hidden within events that seem quite normal. An old friend turned up; you came upon a book; a new job obligated you to reexamine your goals, and you discovered that earning more money did not satisfy you.

Consider the many people that God has woven into your life throughout your time here on earth. Consider the grandparents, or even the great-grandparents, who impacted your spiritual development, whether you personally knew them or not! Perhaps an early impression of your grandparents has always been just a few thoughts away from your conscious thinking. Consider the impact of the spiritual journey that your parents have taken, and the spiritual issues that they directly or indirectly wrestled with, regardless of whether they were Christians. All the words you overheard or that were unconsciously registered in your mind — they all amount to something! God begins very early in our life to pose God-sized questions, and has created within us a sincere search for answers.

A doctor takes a stethoscope to listen in on the physical life of the unborn, developing child. If we could listen in on the *spiritual* life of the unborn child, what would it sound like? Early in our lives, we ask the question, *Where did the world come from?* The parents, who may have grown numb to such fundamental questions, now join their child in contemplating the possibility that God made the world. Our souls are made in such a way that even early in our lives we search for the meaning of life.

Evangelism 101

When I was 12, we attended a little Bible church down the road. Pastor Denny was a follower of the Jack Hyles school of Bible teaching. I was at the beginning of my faith journey, wide-eyed and naive. Our method of evangelism was to knock on a door in a neighborhood and wait for someone to answer. We received guidance in grooming, smiling, and courage. The method was to say these words to that person: "If you died today, would you go to Heaven or Hell?"

I remember the house. The cement steps were crooked, the screen was torn, leaves were spilling over the gutters. The man was old; I guessed, in my seasoned 12 years of life, that he was likely 50. He opened the door, and I said, "If you died today, would you go to Heaven or Hell?" There was a pause. The man looked me in the eyes and said, "Son, I don't know the answer to your question, but if you don't get off my porch you're gonna find out." I sort of sensed something didn't go quite well but I wasn't sure. I told my story at the round-up time and was praised for courage. In His time and space, God blesses and chooses not to bless some things, including our best efforts.

Another method was to visit bars at night — the ones with rusty pickup trucks (always with gun racks) and no paving in the parking lot. At around 12 or 13 years old, I was invited along on this night mission of "special ops" forces. (I'm not sure my parents really knew the whole picture — but, hey, it's a church event and Allan was invited!) The method was to go to the bar around 11 pm and begin to preach through a bullhorn, out in the dirt parking lot. I gathered that the men in that bar didn't respect or appreciate our courage and our pure motive of fixing their souls. A man wearing camouflage and a beard walked out of the bar, wobbling a bit, held up a gun, and said (I quote), "Get the hell out of here — *now*!!!" We ran back to our station wagons and reflected, out loud, "Such God haters!"

God can bless our ridiculous efforts. Even after we butcher the Gospel and His glory, *still* God will choose to bless our frail, self-absorbed methods.

Pastor Denny asked me if I wanted to become a bus captain. I said okay. My sales territory would be a trailer park in Taneytown Md. Every Saturday I would go visit and tell people that a bus would come Sunday morning and pick up their children and take them to church. They always said yes; they didn't ask me my name and serial number, or do a background check on me. As I visited these children, I was exposed to shocking humanity. Men would answer the trailer door in their "wife beater" shirts and boxers, hear the words, "I'll take your children," and they would answer, "The kids will be ready." The trailers were full of cigarette smoke and fried food smells and barking dogs and matted shag carpet. The kids were usually ready Sunday morning at 8 am. Our old bus was loud enough to signal our arrival. Many of the kids dressed themselves as their parents or step parents slept, often sleeping off hangovers. The kids called me Pastor Al; I was 13.

This was the beginning of my calling. I began to love those children. I remember stepping over big, snoring, passed-out men to reach my arms out to a waiting four-year-old. Each week a different child was allowed to sit with me on the front seat of the bus. If you came to church, you got a free McDonald's hamburger, and I would buy the fries myself with the money I had earned working at local farms. If you got converted and came forward at the altar call, you got a free, brand new Bible, presented in front of everyone on the bus. Someone got saved every week, and we had the Bible presentation for each of them.

In my self-involved middle-class educated mind, it's easy now to look down on these people — as well as the church that reached out to them. But even here, God can work and move. God uses what He uses, in His time and space, without our approval. This flawed, silly, pay-you-to-get saved model was my crucible of call into the ministry at age 13. I loved those children and they loved me. I still miss them.

Effectual calling

> "Effectual calling is the work of God's Spirit,
> whereby: Convincing us of our sin and misery,
> Enlightening our minds in the knowledge of Christ,
> and Renewing our wills, He doth persuade and
> enable us to embrace Jesus Christ, freely offered to us
> in the Gospel."
>
> — Westminster Shorter Catechism, #31

I remember being asked to visit a dying man, the father of a member of my congregation. He had consistently rejected anything that had to do with his personal relationship with God. He had resisted the efforts of his family, and even the most articulate and dedicated ministers that God had brought into his life, and there seemed to have been quite a number of them. Yet one thing became very clear to me: this man was not ignorant about spiritual issues! His eyes said, "I'm ready to talk," while his body told me, "We're almost done here!" His voice was broken and humble.

Whenever I came to see him, we would talk about construction work. He was a residential home contractor, and I had been involved in that line of work for most of my life. We would talk about how the methods of residential construction had changed, and I was impressed with the analytical mind that God had given this man. At each visit we would again talk about carpentry and construction, but I would always end by holding his hand and praying for him. I remember well the feel of his leathery, calloused grip against the surface of my wimpy preacher hands. Each time, tears came to his eyes and we exchanged a warm good-bye. At about the fifth visit, this man looked at me and told me that he needed to get ready to meet God. We then shared some scripture together, and then, in a childlike way, he said the sinner's prayer. God's grace defined this moment that had eternal consequences.

Reflecting on this scene causes us to ask the questions, *How did that conversion experience take place?* Did this man first encounter God with my visits? Was that analytical mind of his stuck in neutral concerning spiritual issues, for all the years preceding our meeting at this hospital bed? The answer is emphatically, NO! God had him on a spiritual birth line, and I was privileged to be present at the moment of delivery. God had used many, many people, events, circumstances, and thought processes to bring him to the point of the new birth.

Though an old man, he was a baby in Christ after a very long pregnancy. Praise the Lord for all those who labored in prayer over this man's soul, years before I even met him! Furthermore, if we look closely at this dear man's conversion experience, we can see a pattern that God has, time and time again, drawn in the lives of His children. Who was most important in the long pregnancy period? Certainly it could not have taken place without the implanted seed of truth! After the seed was planted, who was the most important messenger or cultivator along the way? We are tempted to conclude that I must have been more able or articulate that all who had gone before me. But I happened to arrive at the moment when he was ready to listen with new ears.

Archibald Alexander (writing in 1841) provides a colorful picture of this conversion process, in *Thoughts on Religious Experience* — part of a 20-volume work:

> It may be justly and scripturally compared to a growing crop: after the seed is sown it vegetates, we know not how, and then it receives daily the sun's influence, and from time to time refreshing showers; but about the time of harvest, after a long drought, there comes a plentiful shower, by means of which, nutriment is afforded for the formation of the full corn in the ear. No one will dispute the importance and efficacy of this last shower in maturing the grain; but had there been no cultivation and no showers long before, this had never produced any effect.

So, conversion is a process. God used all of the people and circumstances of this man's life, including the threat of death, to bring him to a point of personal commitment to Christ, and I was the individual who appeared at the time of harvest. Others had labored long and hard to share the Gospel and had been an example to him for many, many years! The vital point to consider is this: preceding the event of spiritual birth, there is a long pregnancy period, where God uses many voices and vehicles to call His children to a point of embracing Jesus as their Savior.

Spiritual "midwife"

Steve Smallman reminds us that "we are not called to be salesmen for Jesus, trying to 'close the deal' no matter what it takes; we are called to be spiritual midwives, available and ready to help with the birth." If we can grasp the whole Biblical teaching behind this lesson on the birth line, many doorways into becoming a more effective evangelist and disciple will begin to appear.

I believe that many of the "confrontational dialogue" chains of bondage are destroyed when we apply the truths of the birth line. We begin to be freed from the tensions and the quandary of how to relate to people who don't yet believe. What value do we give them, if any? We begin to recognize our own presumptuous attitudes. God had *each of us* on a schedule and a birth line, and, in like manner, He has others on a schedule! The point at which people commit their lives to Jesus is most often the conclusion of a long string of divine events.

If we can see that God has planned and initiated the pregnancy and all of the influences that sustains that growing spiritual life, our method and philosophy of sharing our faith will change. Our role moves from authorizing the germination of the spiritual life, to being a midwife or encourager to an event that is beyond our control. The style of Evangelical Christianity that is constantly pushing people toward salvation in order to get them "converted" — manipulating them with music, repeated invitations, or a sort of sales routine — is an ugly deformity of Christian practice that results in bad doctrine. This does not mean that we avoid confronting people with the truth, but that it must always be combined with a listening, respectful ear. This kind of pressure is better than disguising the Gospel for those who do not believe.

God does use our warm and persuasive presentation of the Gospel, but on His timing and not ours! Seeing that our ministry to others is carried out in the context of a "birth line" can release us to a type of ministry that places value on the pregnancy period as well as on the time of birth. The challenge of revealing the "secrets of the kingdom" to people with closed eyes and calloused hearts is most often a slow process. People who become followers of Jesus and stay committed to Him for the long term often move toward Christian belief slowly, step by step and stage by stage.

The birthing experience

When a child is born, it is usually in the context of a mother struggling to allow the baby to be born. "Push"

98

takes on a whole new meaning here. Once born, the child senses the dramatic change of environment and will react with crying that brings a soulful smile to everyone's face in the delivery room. This is very similar to the spiritual kind of birth, as well. The moment surrounding the time of conversion can be full of effort and emotionally charged — understandably, considering the significance of the spiritual birth! The conversion experience can often be remembered in detail, clearly placed on the map and the calendar. Whenever someone is asked about her spiritual life, there is comfort in being able to share the specific day and place where she trusted in Jesus as her Savior.

All spiritual births are not the same. Many of God's children enter the kingdom of God with little or no emotion associated with this eternal event. The reality of the new birth is not proven by knowing a specific date, but it is shown in a dynamic faith that trusts wholly in Jesus Christ. God works in many ways, as the hearts of mankind are kneaded and nurtured by the work of His spirit. Those who have placed their trust in Jesus, regardless of the circumstances surrounding their birth into the kingdom, are truly the sons and daughters of God!

Knowing that God works in people's lives through many different experiences and on many different schedules releases the Christian to effect his word for Christ in countless ways. The journey to Christ is a process, not just an event. One of our most common mistakes is to try to do it all at once. We wait for an opportunity to share our faith with a friend or acquaintance, and when the opportunity comes, we unload the whole message and even call for a decision. Few people are ready for that; and, far more often than not, the attempt results in polarization rather than in faith. Jesus taught that coming to faith is a process (John 4:38). It is not always harvest time, but it is always time for something: planting, cultivating, watering, or harvesting. It can be a relief to realize that we are only part of a process.

God has orchestrated our lives so that we meet different kinds of people who have an authentic relationship with Him. Perhaps we encounter God through their prayers at dinnertime, or the Christmas cards that reveal that Christ means something real to them. People who become part of our life's crises, accomplishments, and questions can be used in a powerful way to nurture a spiritual appetite in our souls! If we dare to take time and reflect upon the pregnancy period of our own conversion experiences, we bein to recognize a profound web of people, circumstances and encounters. If God has worked through others' lives to reach us, the question we must now ask is: *How is He working through* my *life to reach other people?*

God can use us in a myriad of ways to nurture, cultivate, and ripen the implanted seed of truth in the heart of the people He has placed in our lives. One of the men in a class I lead, often reticent about speaking in front of others, asked if he could share a recent incident that changed his way of thinking. Gary has an office in downtown Washington, DC. He is in the advertising business. Every week, if not every day, a certain homeless man would approach him and ask him for money or try to engage him in conversation. Gary described his normal attitude as "rather fed up with this guy," and he would often walk a block or two out of his way just to avoid him. (This never happens to us — does it?) This man never seemed to change, and instead of trying to improve himself was always asking for something!

During the week following our class discussion of the spiritual birth line, the same scenario unfolded. Gary was walking to this office, only to be approached by this homeless man. As Gary described this incident, he related how his view of this man was transformed. No longer was this man a nuisance. Gary realized that God had this homeless man on a different birth line schedule than his own. This man had been brought into Gary's life as a target of his ministry! The thoughts, seeds of kindness, and truth that he could share with this homeless man might contribute to the progress of his birth line. Gary said, *"A light went on. This man now had value, and I could see a new role I could play in his life!"*

If we look carefully at the process of our own conversion experience, we gain a radically new perspective on our witness to others. I know that the perception that others are "in process" has revolutionized the way I think about people, and has released me to minister to them *where they are*. There is no single meaningful moment for this ministry: the time of spiritual birth is not the "only" meaningful encounter with others. God can use us in myriad ways to nurture, cultivate, and ripen the implanted seed of truth in the hearts of the people He has placed in our lives — a process of cultivation that may be beyond our own ability to fully detect.

Two Stories: two spiritual birthlines

Nelson's conversion experience

Introduction: I am 42 years old and have attended church since before its beginnings. I have lived in Northern Virginia almost all my life. I am the second of two children born to an "older couple." My father spent time working for the federal government. My mother was a wife and mother, never working outside of the home. We were raised in the Episcopal Church (my mother's denomination). Between my birth and graduation from high school, my family moved only once.

Life Influences: My father's family was from Maryland. My grandfather was born in Germany, and my grandmother was born in the USA. My father's family was from Lutheran background, and my grandmother and uncle were very involved with their church.

My mother was from Georgia and met my father while he attended Georgia Tech. My mother trained at a secretarial school. She was raised by her grandmother since birth, because her mother died when she was only one week old. My mother was not a well person, being born with petit-mal (a lesser form of epilepsy). My mother was raised Episcopal and did not know a day she didn't hold the Lord as her Savior.

My parents were married 12 years before my brother was born, and therefore he was the jewel in their crown. I arrived seven weeks early, and was not the choice to save if a choice had to be made. I never truly "felt" loved. My brother was artistic, and was coddled and protected by my mother. I was viewed as being independent, responsible, and resourceful and therefore I could take care of myself.

My mother spent many years in and out of the hospital. Through it all her faith never wavered, never weakened. I remember, near the end of her life, an episode that struck me as odd. I overheard my mother talking with my father about the fact that she was dying, and she said "I don't care what will happen to me. I know I am going home. I just wish I could spend more time with *you*."

There was never any question of Dad remarrying. There had been only one woman for him, and with her he weathered all kinds of storms. My mother died when I was 16. She had an experience on her deathbed that my father was witness to and which we believe was repeated 22 years later with my brother's death. Near death, she began to talk quietly to someone. My father kneeled down to hear what she was saying. She put her hand on his head and said, "See, God, this is my husband, please take care of him." She smiled and then slipped into a coma.

I went away to college five days after I graduated from high school. It was the first time that I was on my own, the first time I was responsible for no one but myself. It was a rocky road. I dropped out for a year and returned home to work. But mainly I was typical of the era. From the age of 17 to 24, I was a drug addict. Someone once asked me if I'm not being harsh on myself, but I know and God knows that I'm being honest.

When I was 21, my brother became a Christian. Many things he did wrong from the start, especially alienating my father by "writing him off." I saw the hurt it caused and wanted no part of a religion that did that to someone. Through all this, I began to read a Bible he gave me and went line by line through John. I would write him these long letters filled with questions, but he never wrote back. Whenever I returned home I would out of support go to church with him. There I met people who were truly interested in me. They never preached, never (openly) judged; they loved me. It was this love that broke through to the person who was starving inside.

But still I remained in my life and lifestyle. I had this notion that I had to get "clean" before I could turn to Christ to "get right with God." I knew there was more to life than what I was feeling inside. There was emptiness inside me that drugs, alcohol, sex, or whatever thrill would not fill.

By my senior year I lived off campus, and due to the interruption in my education, I was older than most seniors (at 24). I do remember one psalm sticking in my mind about how I felt. It is Psalm 32. To this day in my Bible, I have written next to this psalm, *my witness psalm of my conversion.*" The verses that kept haunting me were long. "For day and night your hand was heavy upon me; my strength was sapped . . . but it was like running on a treadmill" — I couldn't get the notion out of my mind that someone was catching up to me, but I was afraid to look back and see who it was.

One day, in August 1975, I returned to school to get ready for the fall term. I spent five hours alone in the car with my thoughts, returning after spending time with my family and with some families from my brother's church. This persistent feeling that I was being followed and watched kept creeping up on me. Finally I pulled up to the house I lived in, one of three apartments occupied by drug users and dealers. All my resolve dissolved just by walking into the lobby. By the time I was in the apartment I shared with my girlfriend, I was back at step one: high and disappointed with myself and my weak resolve.

I remember walking into the bathroom and doing the unthinkable: I looked at myself in the mirror. But this time I wasn't alone. I now "saw" whose hand was heavy upon me, as it says in Psalm 32. Behind me was Jesus showing me His mirror — what He saw when He looked in it at me. It was an image I couldn't handle. I had been trying to get myself right before I met Him where He was — and in turn He told me that He would meet me where I was. It wasn't that I had to stop the sin before I came to Him, but I had to acknowledge my sin, and He removed the physical burden of my sin and through Him I had the strength to change paths and walk with Him.

As I weaned myself, everyone I had lived with and partied with became suspicious. My friends wanted no part of the "new me." What finally broke me from the old life was actually graduating and returning home to live. I became involved in my brother's church and settled into a new life. Once in a while the old life would call up or visit. Each time the Lord would use these times to show me that light truly has nothing in common with darkness. — *Nelson G.*

Richard's conversion experience

Introduction: I'm a 31-year-old freelance writer and an ordained Baptist minister and seminary professor. Essentially, I don't recall a time when I didn't believe in the facts of Jesus' earthly existence. My parents were both Christians, strong and committed in the faith, but my father in particular was aware that each person has to come to an understanding of Christ on his own.

Life influences: During high school, I was clearly searching for a spiritual grounding that I did not get in the Baptist Church that I attended as a youth. I studied most of the world's major religions, particularly eastern religions. I did extensive reading in the scriptures of Hinduism and Buddhism, and, although I never adopted them officially, a number of my friends later told me that they fully expected such a conversion. During this period, however, I still read the Bible from time to time and maintained an interest in Christianity to a degree.

After graduating from high school, I lost interest in religion initially. Eventually I ended up back in California, where I attended Humboldt State University and commuted home to the Bay Area on most weekends. It was at this point that I began a very intense reexamination of Christianity. I experienced a profound depression, and this in turn led to an examination of my life as a whole. One day I came into class and it was a lecture on the American theologian Jonathan Edwards. The only way I can describe my reaction to the lectures on Edwards was that I was stunned. I was simply enchanted with the brilliance of Edwards's mind and the clarity of his theology. The professor taught us that

Edwards was a Calvinist, and I thought that if Jonathan Edwards was a Calvinist, then I needed to reexamine my opinion of Calvin.

I went to the college library and checked out John Calvin's *Institutes of the Christian Religion*. I checked Calvin's assertions against the Biblical verses that he quoted, and I was amazed to find that Calvinism was simply another name for the theology of the Bible. From there, I decided that a rereading of the Bible was in order. The method that I used was to simply read the text and ignore everything that I had been taught about it, simply letting God speak to me through the text. God used the experience to change my life. I came away from that reading as a convinced Christian and a convinced Calvinist.　　— *Richard A.*

Chapter 7

The Age of Shaking

Built a church today and all shouted Amen,
Now never never be nomads again.
Nice seats, stained glass, all real clean,
Pastor's office for the souls to be seen.
People fill our church, it's a thrill to see them gather
So, now, what's the matter?
People don't come from some lonely door.
They come from that other Church, they don't like it
no more.

— Al Dayhoff, *Build it and they will come*

I was sitting outside the little rented beach apartment on
Fort Myers beach; this was off season, a Florida August.
The small room was musty and damp; the shower didn't
drain, rain came in through the windows, and ants made
daily raids, blowing their tiny bugles as they gained new
territory. I informed them that my bed was off limits. But I
loved the place: it was perfect for reading and writing.

At 6 a.m. I made a cup of coffee and went to sit on the
beach, in a splintery old Adirondack chair about 50 feet
from the waves. There was something different in the
scenery that morning. Six fresh roses, banded together, had
been left lying in the sand. I had to wonder: Did these
wash ashore last night? Why would someone leave half a
dozen new roses on the beach? Was love made, or lost, at

this spot? Six roses (I am told) means, "I love you, I miss you." Twelve means, "Be my steady." And 24 means, "You're always on my mind."

The morning walkers came along in ones, twos, threes, and all of them stopped, or just pointed, and debated what might have happened at that spot. "Someone proposed — and she said no!" "A fight broke out and the roses were left behind." "They were just too drunk to remember to take the roses home."

I felt like an anthropologist, studying human evolutionary development. The level of interest from strangers was striking; there was laughter, and there was silent, pensive gazing. Sometimes their body language said that they had come upon sacred ground. Others reacted as if their casual morning stroll had broken onto an emotional crime scene. But *no one* disturbed the flowers. Parents gripped little curious hands, preventing their children from touching the roses as they passed by.

There was one exception. A youngish couple, probably in their thirties, strolled up and stopped at the flowers. His hair blowing in the wind was as long as hers; she wore a wispy wrapped tie-dyed dress. They had that free sort of hippie look that I would love to acquire in about 20 years (if my wife, Deb, would join me!). The young man immediately got down on one knee in a silly-serious way and handed her a flower. She was quiet, blushing, smiley — obviously pleased.

As the morning continued, there were more beach walkers and more comments. Single women joggers would always slow their pace and look back. Single men didn't seem notice the roses at all.

Suddenly, the lazy morning was interrupted by yelling. An impressive string of cuss words was coming faster than my ants' marching legs. Trees were blocking my view to the left as the sound got louder. I listened for any new cuss words, maybe invented right there on my watch. Finally, the source of the tirade stepped into view. It was the same young man who had presented the single rose to his lady friend — but now he was in a vein-popping, screaming rant, as he sauntered over to the spot where those roses lay. His hands were raised in the air, both middle fingers pointing to the sky.

His free-spirited girlfriend now appeared, walking slowly, 100 feet behind him. She was not surrendering; she was speaking to him, though he obviously couldn't hear her words. He stomped over to the remaining five roses and drop-kicked them into the air, before stomping away. The petals broke free of their stems and fluttered down slowly down to the wet sand — a shower of petals as if for a wedding, to adorn the happy couple as they take off for their life together. Now the young woman stopped walking and exhaled loudly, a sigh that signaled that something was over. Maybe it was the end of their light-hearted walk on the beach, or maybe it was the end of the relationship. The angry young man had already walked almost out of eyesight, and she was not trying to catch up with him.

Such drama, just a few hours after sunrise — you couldn't pay for such a show! I was expecting the lights would come up and the usher to announce that the matinee was over. But not quite. A family with a small, wandering five-year-old girl came up. Her blonde curls bounced as she rushed over, full of silliness, to collect as many rose petals as she could before her parents stopped her. She collected a bright handful of the soft red playthings, happily holding their beauty, tight and gentle, in her hands. I wondered if she understood that the petals would soon shrivel and harden. And now the tide was then coming in. The remaining petals were snatched away by the fingertips of the waves. It was 7:45 am.

We who live in the West enjoy our trips to the beach. The morning sun affirms our unquestioned sense of safety and freedom. We are able to enjoy the beauty all around us, unfettered, while we sip a three-shot-extra-hot mocha. Christianity is protected by the constitution and by the Judeo-Christian ethic that undergirds our institutions. We assume it will always be there, fixed, strong, unmoving. Yes, we have had our share of struggle: foreign wars, political brawls, economic ups and downs. There has been suffering in our own lives, and heartaches, too many to count. Yet, today, we seem to be in new uncharted territory, and a message of "something is coming" is being spoken by every political stripe and school of thought. It's worth asking: "What time is it?"

It's 7:45 am in the western world. Something steady and strong is now shaking, and it's not just another fictional "end of the world" movie that entertains us and then it's over; we get into our safe cars, drive back to our homes, and get into our ant-free beds. Something is shaking, and it's getting the attention of the elderly folks who have "been there, done that" in their years on this earth. The middle class — the backbone of our economy, civic safety, moral bearings, and optimism — is whispering even louder: "Something is shaking." The college grads who worked hard, went into debt, and are hoping to be rewarded with a job and new opportunities are blogging: "Something is shaking." Our youth, whom we crave to protect from evil and harm, are being held by parents who are trying to hide their own fears, but they are mouthing the words: "Something is shaking." The very institutions that uphold our society — financial, civic, military, educational, health, and religious — are now visibly shaking.

I am often described as a quiet optimist. I find that waiting things out tends to bring the desired reward. It's a muscle my dad had, that shows up in my own story. I'm not a doomsdayer; I see the cycles in history. Peace is followed by war, and war is often followed by another war or another stretch of peace. Dictators rise and threaten the world, dress up in military costumes, and finally get overthrown or die, either badly or in disgrace. A new virus appears, the guys in white coats get all giddy and stop shaving, and they finally emerge with vials in their hands that save the day. A set of giant skyscrapers in New York City falls down, 3,000 people die. We gasp in horror — but then a new building is built, a freedom memorial is designed, and we are back to business, sobered and wiser.

Ants invade our homes and set up their colonies in secret passageways, and we call the bug man. Job finished, and we are all better.

I have always viewed the world from a safe place, never expecting that all the shaking would get anywhere close to me, my kids, or my world. In my many mission trips to Africa and Asia, we would go boldly into the crazy chaos and even delight in it. (I recall the herd of warthogs that blocked my hut door in Ghana, and the dangerous riot in Nairobi.) But I always knew I would get on a plane and return to the Starbucks near my home, where they know I like my two-pump mochas, extra hot. I've always had the abundance of safety, food, and health, and the opportunity to ponder complacently the chaos in other places.

Now I watched from my splintery Adirondack chair as the six roses came apart and eventually washed out to sea. The roses seem hard to find right now, as we try to rewind the story of Western civilization, with all its safety and opportunity. Our civilization was built on the Judeo-Christian ethic, of trust in God and concern for one another. Have we lost that foundation? Along with the decline of the Judeo-Christian ethic has come a fracturing at every level. When Bill Cosby goes from being a father-figure to a monster, who can we trust?

So — *what exactly is shaking?*

Our bodies are shaking

> The U.S. is now in the grip of a full-blown obesity epidemic.

* More than 35% of U.S. adults are obese.
* By 2030, that rate could reach 44% — *in every state.*
* These obesity rates mean poor health.
* Adults with severe obesity lose 8–10 years of life expectancy, a rate comparable to life-long smokers.
* Obesity has been linked to: hypertension, coronary heart disease, diabetes, stroke, gallbladder disease, osteoarthritis, sleep apnea, respiratory problems, endometriosis, breast, prostate and colon cancers, breathlessness, asthma, reproductive hormone abnormalities, impaired fertility and other problems.

More than 30% of our children and teens are either overweight or obese, resulting in the loss of 1.5 *million* years of life (American Heart Association research).

Our economy is shaking

Like many other Americans, I am asking myself, "Can I ever retire?" What will it take to win the footrace I'm running, between the time I have in a young body, able to work, and the approaching time when I am unable to work? Money spells the trajectory of many important things — like healthcare, bridges, policemen, and E.coli bacteria inspections. The time has arrived for the "come to Jesus meeting," between dwindling resources and pressing basic needs.

* In 1980, the U.S. national debt was less than 1 trillion dollars; today, it is rapidly approaching 17 trillion dollars.
* In 1970, the total amount of debt in the United States (government debt + business debt + consumer debt, etc.) was less than 2 trillion dollars; today it is over 56 trillion dollars.
* According to the *Economist*, the United States was the best place in the world to be born into — in 1988. Today, the United States is tied for 16th place.
* Since 2001, more than 56,000 manufacturing facilities in the United States have been permanently shut down. In fourteen years!
* According to the New York Times, Detroit has approximately 70,000 abandoned buildings.
* When NAFTA was pushed through Congress in 1993, the United States had a trade *surplus* with Mexico of 1.6 billion dollars. By 2010, we had a trade *deficit* with Mexico of 61.6 billion dollars.
* Back in 1985, our trade deficit with China was approximately 6 million dollars. In 2012, our trade deficit with China had ballooned to 315 *billion* dollars — the largest trade deficit between two nations in the history of the world.
* More than half — 53 percent — of all American workers make *less* than $30,000 a year.

* In the United States today, the wealthiest one percent of all Americans have a greater net worth than the bottom 90 percent combined.

Overall, the federal government runs nearly 80 different "means-tested welfare programs," and at this point more than 100 million Americans are enrolled in at least one of them.

* U.S. families with a head of household under the age of 30 have a poverty rate of 37 percent.
* According to one calculation, the number of Americans on food stamps now exceeds the combined populations of 25 states.
* In 1967, one out of every 20 Americans was on Medicaid. Today, one out of every 6 Americans is on Medicaid.
* In Miami, 45% of all children are living in poverty, as are more than 50% in Cleveland and almost 60% in Detroit.

Today, more than one million public school students in the United States are homeless. This is the first time that has ever happened in our history.

Our education system is shaking

In 2011, the Nation's Report Card (NAEP, 2011) summarized where we are.

* Two out of three eighth-graders can't read proficiently — and most of them will never catch up.

117

* Nearly two-thirds of eighth-graders scored below proficient in math.
* Nearly three-fourths of 8th and 12th grade students cannot write proficiently.
* An *Education Week* report in 2012 found some progress in the numbers of graduating high school students, but —
* More than one million students drop out of school every year.
* For African-American and Hispanic students across the country, dropout rates are close to 40% (compared to the national average of 27%).

After World War II, the United States had the #1 high school graduation rate in the world. Today, according to an OECD report, we have dropped to # 22, among the 27 industrialized nations.

* American students rank 14th in reading, 17th in science, and 25th in math (out of 27).
* 13 other countries have a greater percentage of 25–34 year-olds who have completed some college.
* Over the course of his working life, an American male with a college degree can expect to earn nearly $675,000 more; an American female $340,000 more — a much greater differential than in any other country.

In order to earn a decent wage in today's economy, most students will need at least some postsecondary education (according to a 2012 report by the United States Department of Labor).

* Americans who earn a college degree make a 40 percent higher salary than those with just a high school diploma.
* The share of jobs in the U.S. economy needing a college degree will increase to 63% in the next decade, or 22 million new employees with college degrees. At the current pace, we will fall at least 3 million college degrees short.

For workers without a high school diploma, the future is bleak.

* Nearly 44 percent of dropouts under age 24 are jobless.
* The unemployment rate of high school dropouts older than 25 is more than three times that of college graduates.
* High school dropouts can expect to earn just 5 percent of what a typical high school graduate will make, over the course of his or her lifetime (College Board Advocacy & Policy Center, 2010).

Despite sustained unemployment, employers are finding it difficult to hire Americans with adequate basic skills, and experts expect this problem to intensify.

* More than 75 percent of employers report that new employees with four-year college degrees

lacked "excellent" basic knowledge and applied skills.

* Nearly half of those who employed recent *high school graduates* said overall preparation was "deficient."

Lots more discouraging details can be found in the following resources: *Getting Ahead* (Business Roundtable, 2009); *An Economy that Works* (McKinsey & Company, 2011); *Are They Really Ready to Work?* (The Conference Board); *Help Wanted: Projections of Jobs and Economic Requirements through 2018* (Georgetown Center on Education and the Workforce, 2010).

Our food supply is shaking

I have been often guilty of a self-righteous attitude when it comes to weight control. But it occurred to me one day that my abundant grocery store, just a mile from my house, has a counterpart in many neighborhoods — as a fast food restaurant or just a convenience store. You would have to walk for seven hours straight to burn off a lunch of a super-sized Coke, fries, and a Big Mac. U.S. Surgeon General David Satcher labeled fast food "a major contributor to the obesity epidemic."

* Each day, 1 in 4 Americans visits a fast food restaurant.
* Americans spend more than $110 *billion* a year on fast food.

* In 2009, the fast food industry spent more than $4 billion dollars on advertising.
* The impact of our fast food habits on the next generation is catastrophic.
* One in every three children born in the year 2000 will develop diabetes in their lifetime.
* In the menu items purchased by children and teens, 30% of the calories are from sugar and saturated fat.
* Children and teenagers consume on average more than 64 *gallons* of soft drinks per year.
* McDonald's distributes more toys per year than Toys-R-Us.

Our churches are shaking

The actual rate of church attendance from head counts is much lower than the 40% reported in polls — probably less than 20%. Researchers in 2004 performed actual counts of people attending Christian churches (Catholic, mainline Protestant, and evangelical) and found that just 17.7% of the population attended a Christian church on any given weekend. Sociologists C. Kirk Hadaway and Penny Long Marler found similar results: 52 million people attend church, not 132 million (which would be 40%) (*Journal for the Scientific Study of Religion*, 2005).

We can all see the shaking that surrounds us. Shootings. The cost of health care. So many, many people on disability. Surveillance everywhere we go, identity theft. Pornography grabs hold of our men and boys; marriages disintegrate. Shaking, shaking, shaking. In some parts of Detroit, trees are growing up through the asphalt of the roads.

Let's be clear: this shaking is not something that the world has never before known. Other centuries have known disease, war, and poverty; plagues, crusades, and religious inquisitions; volcano eruptions and tsunamis. America has been spared from most such catastrophes — but now something is shaking. Whether there have been five or twenty-three civilizations in history, some commentators say that the West is now experiencing a new, historically documented shaking.

I believe it is shaking deep in the bellows of the soul. Projections show that our current generation of youth will die earlier, have less money, work longer, see more suicides, have fewer Job opportunities, and endure more physical disability than previous generations. Shaking leads to more shaking — and something collapses.

Did the West throw away the roses on the beach? Maybe we assumed that the comforts, resources, and heroes of the Western civilization were unshakable. Or that they could be easily replaced with something new, shiny, better than ever. Not anymore. As the ground under our feet shakes, the vibrations travel up through the institutions and into our everyday lives. This shaking, this moment of nervous awkwardness, creates an unspoken fear in all of us. It shakes our norms, our security blankets, our stashed safety accounts.

And this fear makes space for eternity. It is a true statement that we don't need God until we *need God*.

Amid the growing uncertainty, we have to ask a hard question: *"Will the Church matter?"* Has the time come for the Western church to find a new reformation for a new era? Has a stern schoolmaster arrived on the scene, to strip away our petty distractions — the infighting, the moralism, the theological superiority complexes and silly hang-ups, the epicurean comforts of mochas served at church? *Will a new generation of mission-driven believers rise from the shaking?*

God tells us the shaking has purpose. This a time for the evangelist in all of us to be aware of where *we* are, so we are prepared speak to the soul who is searching for a home that is not made with human hands. Shaking gives us the opportunity to speak about eternity. But those conversations must start with relationships. Our ministry must venture outside our comfortable but shrinking churches: *outpost ministry* rather than pulpit ministry.

It's our time to listen, to hear, to be present, and to share the historic Christian faith, that Jesus died and rose again for mankind and individuals like you and me. We only have one unshakeable Presence, and that is God Himself.

> My heart is in anguish within me,
> And the terrors of death have fallen upon me.
> Fear and trembling come upon me;
> And horror has overwhelmed me.

> Psalm 55:4

Chapter 8

The Image of God is Speaking

All I got is questions
Got no answers I like
Never know why, never know who
All I got is questions
Never seen no light
Never know why, never know who
Same questions, all night

— C. Selgin, *Same Damn Questions*

I went to Las Vegas with my buddy Chris. It was January of 2013; he had a builder's conference to go to and needed some company. I had never seen the movie *Dumb and Dumber* — just the thought of "sin city" had kept it off my must-see list. But here was Chris, with a plane ticket for me and a place to stay. I said what any man raised in a religious fundamentalist home would say: Sure, I'm in!

I had a cartoon image of what the city would look like, smell like and act like at 6 in the morning. But the cartoons in my head didn't really capture the strange planet of Las Vegas, all the escaping suburban inmates stretching their freedom for one last night before returning to their prison cells: the work cubicle, the responsibilities, the traffic, the middle age crisis, and all the rest of "back home." The swirling mass of food vendors under gyrating florescent colors and pulsing neon signs, the opulence and noise of the casinos, and the herds of people heading to unknown adventures while staring at their smart phones — the racket quickly shut down most of my senses.

But an inner rebellion began deep inside me. It was as if some other being was living in my "man cave," the cave *inside* me. I gathered my courage and talked some sense to that voice from within: I'm in charge here, so just lay off and wait for my instructions. And I got my answer: "Give it your best shot, baby, but we didn't sign up for this detail." Something in this place was very wrong for my inner being. I was in the wrong place and watching the wrong people, still trying to stay unaffected by the humanity all around me. Since I don't gamble, I had figured it would be safe to just stand by and watch the people who do, telling myself, "I'll never be as stupid as these people." Even worse, not all of the humanity was here to play. Every ten feet or so, someone holding a sign looked me in the eyes. "Out of work please help," "hungry," "my kids thank you." Or maybe, "Take a picture with Elvis." And then there were the ones who couldn't hold up a sign even if they wanted to.

The immense size of these casinos boggled the mind. I couldn't see the beginning or the end. Dinging noises and blinking signs were everywhere. To simply walk through these places, you had to somehow turn down the sensors and microphones built into your body. It was a loud, bright, windowless village. You could gamble, eat, sleep, get a pedicure, smoke, dance all night, get Starbucks coffee and every other kind of beverage as well. You could be vacationing or working, do your taxes or meditate, and never leave these places.

And many, apparently, had never left. The elderly people in walkers and wheelchairs at the slot machines smacked me in my self-righteousness. I was smugly looking down on the drunks and out-of-control middle-aged men going wild, but these people barely able to walk jolted me, my eyes got watery. One dear man could not get from his slot machine to the bathroom — so he did what he had to do, right there where he was, and people just moved away from him as if it happened all the time. It didn't seem to faze anyone, and a staff member eventually showed up and seemed to know the routine.

Here I was, 52 years old, and I was hoping my mother would never find out I came here — half afraid that she would suddenly show up. "Mom! What are *you* doing here???" I kept walking and I came to the gambling tables for blackjack and all the other games, with a dealer at the head of each table. At one table, a beautiful woman in a tight, low-cut dress was masterfully playing the men, while the men were playing the odds against the dealer and each other. Laughter switched to anger and back again, 10 times a minute. Everyone was using everyone one else, and everyone was going along with the game.

And did I mention the cameras? The security and the unmarked security. Walking around, watching the security as they watched the cameras. I wondered if the security cameras presented me naked, like the ones at the airport — sweet revenge on the guys looking at me! Then I noticed all the men wearing sunglasses. Of course, those lights *were* laser bright, migraine triggers, no doubt. Or maybe they wore sunglasses to be cool, right? Something I have always craved to be, until my darling teenagers told me, "Dad, please stop, you're *trying too hard.*" (I responded by redoubling my efforts to be cool; it's a work in progress.) No, the sunglasses, I'm told, are to hide the giveaway glances that gamblers can't hide, so other gamblers can't guess the card strength they're holding. Bluffing, retreating, cockiness, disappointment, excitement — these are body language tools that seasoned gamblers can control and feign. I was impressed by how these guys could stay so still, watching through their asphalt-thick sunglasses and putting on good theatre for virgin spectators like me. I stood quietly by my friend Chris, pretending I kind of belonged there. I might never know when to hold them and when to fold them, but I would make the dealer and the casino very happy.

All our scars

Whether or not you are wearing sunglasses, you still must live in the Image of God. The Image of God is the Eternal DNA, the double helix structure, housed in every human being. We can work hard at our profile and image on the outside — but God created the inside, with a voice, mind, and compass for navigating the human experience. A Mustang cannot be a Camaro, and a walrus cannot be a grey parakeet: even if the walrus dresses up like a parakeet, we can see his flippers. The image of God is pressed upon the surface of the soul like a tire tread in soft red clay. I'm not the first person to wonder, "Can someone turn off the image of God?" The questions, whispers, the sense of justice are intrinsic to mankind, and so is the slow burn of seeking answers to God-sized questions. Behind the sunglasses at the gaming table sits a thinking, fragile, seeking, confused, questioning soul. And so they sit all around us in life, gambling.

And there's more behind those sunglasses. There always is. As I write this, I'm sitting near the beach in southwest Florida; every body shape and gender, mostly over the age of 79, is sunbathing. I remember, growing up as a fundamentalist teen, that the teaching on mixed bathing was a point in all spring sermons — no swimming at beach or the pool where girls would show up. Even if the sermon started with Moses and the burning bush, somehow mixed bathing was threaded in as a sin against...well, I'm not sure what, but it was a sin. I remember raising my hand in youth group, as a snarky 14-year-old, and asking if mixed bathing was ok in the family bathroom but not the beach. My buddies and the cute red-headed girl all laughed. The pastor's head heated up and green laser beams struck me; I am still scarred for life, especially at the beach. But, sitting in Florida, I noticed something more serious. For the first time, I noticed the scars on people's bodies. Sure, my biker buddies in the blues bar had scars on their faces and arms (maybe from fights with the biker girls?) — scars that were downright cool and manly. But those guys were wearing clothes, their pressed black leather wardrobes from JCPenney.

On the beach, the scars were exposed. They told stories of knee surgery and hip replacements, heart operations, lung and kidney problems, and some "OMG" scars. One guy had a PICC line still taped to his chest, for his chemo later that week. No body part had been spared, judging from my National Geographic expedition in scars. Necks, backs, limbs. Missing pieces, like parts of noses, ears, faces, or divots in the skin. Colostomy bags—there, I said it. Never mind the plastic surgery archeology. The scars tell a story. But where do the scar owners go to tell their story: the hurts and terrors those scars point to?

In all the surveys and questions we have done, talking with the unchurched, we hear one loud, unmistakable question that comes back at us in unguarded moments. "If your God is so great, why is my life so hard?" For most people, the idea of sin is not an answer. They wonder, why is this God (or Being) picking on me? Ok, I'm bad, but is there an end in sight? People have emotional as well as physical scars, too many to count or even process. They try to soothe themselves with a great airbrush job to hide the inner stitch marks that won't go away. The mother who birthed a stillborn son, the teen with a drunk father who died 10 years ago but still lives in his head, these are suffering people who have learned to hide their scars. When cancer shows up, or another personal tragedy, the soul cries out, "Really??" The elephant in the room, as it relates to the soul coming to faith, is *suffering*.

There's something else here: can I say it? The church as a whole hasn't come to terms with suffering either. As we wail and grind along in our different pain scenarios, we, too, question God's goodness. The unchurched watch the churched in their own personal pain, more closely than we might imagine, through their sunglasses. They hear our reasoning and they detect our sugar coating, our clean apologetics. They pick up on our dualism: happy, happy in public, but sad and tormented in secret. Suffering is damn hard, this genius path used by God to awake and call His dear, dear children into the kingdom, and maybe make them ready to leave this world for a brand new out-of-the wrapper body. Yes, God harnesses even the blackness of death to bring about Life. And I think the non-churched want to be *welcomed* into our suffering. Please hear me, I am not saying suffering in any form is easy, or that it feels right, or that we should act like angels who were just given their first set of wings.

As I sit and write this sentence, I'm pretty obviously scarred myself, two weeks out from a second jaw surgery. I shattered my jaw on a fishing trip, in a freak fall. Love and support came at me from all directions, not just from my church. My blues buddies have all called and visited, and my Jewish surgeon and dentist have called, visited, and texted me. I am simply overwhelmed by the love and care, and their empathy has helped my recovery and well-being. Frankly, I couldn't keep them away. At one of my blues bars I have made a number of African-American friends. The black ladies would soothe me with their words and questions, leaning in to touch and hug me. They let me in as one of their own; it was a felt gift that I can't explain. Sure, "Pastor Al" helps, prays and holds other people in distress — but I am like a cat dangling over rushing water when I am the target of others' concern. It's a great weakness of mine, one that God seems to be writing a blues song about, just for me. Yet, despite my pathetic "never show weakness" mentality, I asked my blues buddies to pray for me. And they did.

Does God hear the prayers of those yet to be Christians? Can He even hear their voices? Does He care, or does He turn away and say, "I never knew you?" Those prayers, given from people who don't claim to be church people or Christians, changed my life. We bonded over prayers and the gift I was given, that they would be charged to pray for Pastor Al. One of my blues friends said, "I don't know how to pray." The words "Yeah you do" came out of my mouth, and he nodded with a smile. You see, the soul is made to talk; it's made to talk to God. When we talk, yell, accuse, or even curse God, the person deep inside us communicates with someone. The Image of God seeks out God in all of us. As Christians, we have been so focused on the "front Narrative" — what people say in our debates — that we haven't heard the "back Narrative," the one where people secretly wish it's all true.

One discovers how the image of God speaks and lives inside of us as we discover who our earthly parents really are. Who doesn't know that moment when you see your dad or mom looking back at you from the bathroom mirror? When we lose our parents, we are left as orphans crying out for someone to hear us. It's a moment for the Image Maker to meet the Image Child. Our cry is deep because we are crying for something deeper, deeper even then our parent's death.

When my father died, at 87 years old, I asked out loud, "God, how could you take him so soon?" I slept by his bed the last four nights of his life, in hospice. I whispered each day, "Dad, it's ok, you can go." I knew he'd be worrying about mom, worrying if there was gas in her car and the windows were closed, and if his secret switch to the water heater was turned on. Then I told him that I had to go home. He had been in a coma for four long days. I drove away, and as I got to the fourth traffic light, the nurse called me. "Your father has passed, Mr. Dayhoff." I loved those nurses; they helped dad die well, and they gave him some dignity too. Then it came: tears like I can't ever remember crying. I sobbed like a dog run over in the middle of the road, half alive, half dead and dying hard. I couldn't see the road any more. I was so angry and hurt and sad my chest hurt, and I started coughing. I pulled over and threw up the hospice food behind Hardees.

There are two reasons why funerals are so somber. It is partly over the tragic loss of the deceased in the casket in front, and it's partly over the thought, "When is *my* turn coming, to be the guy lying up front? Should I have on the blue suit, or my Hawaiian buttondown?" I believe we have lost the awareness that the souls of men and women are alive with spiritual questions, fears and secret yearnings: "Maybe there is a God who made me, designed my path, and waits somewhere for me?" This morning, at a cigar shop, I asked a guy in sunglasses what he thought about church people. He laughed and said, "They live in a fairy tale. They inherit a set of thoughts from their parents, and then try to prove to everyone else they are right — because

133

deep down they fear their religion may not be true." He laughed, and I laughed too. He puffed on his cigar, and I puffed on my cigar. Then he pivoted his sunglasses to the top of his head, and he said, "My dad died two weeks ago; I hope he made it in."

Maybe it was the cigar that clarified the image of God.

My study on the beach wasn't yet finished. I started seeing all the tattoos round me with new eyes. Did these marks on the outside of the body give clues about the inside? I have always wanted a tattoo, but by now my skin is a little less, shall we say, elastic. (Stay tuned; if you tell me I can't get one, I will go right out and get it done.) There were tattoos from World War II, like anchors and other things that I couldn't make out because the skin was not exactly smooth or stationary. On the under-60 group there were skulls and bones and dripping blood, scenes out of a horror carnival booth. It's as if they were saying, "I'm familiar with death and evil, and I can send signals to strangers that I'm not afraid. I have inner strength; I'm living with the power of darkness and it can't stop me — for now."

Then there were the tattoos of people's faces, with dates. These people had died, and people they left behind had written their names and memories over their own hearts. Fathers, brothers, sisters, and, yes, babies. I go where other fools fear to go, so I asked one sun-baked lady, "What does your tattoo mean?" She looked at me and said, "My daughter died in a car crash; that's her." She moved her top over to show me.

"Thanks for telling me," I said.

"Thanks for asking." Then she was gone, and so was I.

Hearing the Image of God: Five Big Questions

What questions are we using to listen to the image of God? I want to share with you my five God-sized questions, and I want you to be the judge of them. Let me invite you to evaluate these questions not only in your seminary class, or around your breakfast table. Let me invite you to try them out on the street, around the Thanksgiving table, on a plane, in a biker's bar, with your young children. Your job may be hard: you must only listen. And maybe your *listening* can break into *hearing*: hearing the image of God, hearing the stories of pain, sounds of an orphan, hearing the seeking side and the haunting words that long for hope. One thing we have discovered is that the longer someone talks, the more they talk themselves *toward* God, not away from Him. Sometimes the "slip" doesn't come until the very end of the survey conversation; other times, it bleeds out in every other word.

I hope you will ask these questions with no plan to answer them, but only to listen, to see if by listening you can hear someone's heartbeat. Hear the Image of God revealed in them. People want to be discovered — not *truthed*.

Let me take a risk here. It's not so hard for most people to believe that someone or something created the world. Its complexity, beauty, and natural mechanisms meet us every waking moment, and maybe every sleeping moment too. But many people, even though they suspect that the world is no accident, prefer to hold their cards close. Why should they let us evangelists into their secret thoughts anyway? Would we respect the room of their secret thoughts, or would we drive a dump truck full of our "truths" into that special room? People are very savvy about the chessboard moves of the church and especially about its evangelizing of their unchurched souls. They have cottoned on to our scripts and our serious role-playing with our practice sparring partners.

Maybe the sign that our listening finally breaks into hearing is when we can truly feel the words we speak — as in, "I am so sorry." At that point, someone has dared to give us a chance to really hear their sorrows and pains, trusting that we won't just revert to our own script. This is the beginning of a faith relationship with many delightful chapters ahead. Yes, the gospel gives us hope beyond and around our sorrows, but pain is real and must be heard. Heard by you and me as we listen to our flock, who may even be the people in the address book of our own cellphone. The church today seems to think that so many people are just pagans who never consider God — never even wonder about the three human questions all souls must ask: "Where did I come from?" "Why am I here?" "What happens after death?" The truth is, everyone comes to the point that is the end of themselves and the beginning of God, even if it comes at the moment of physical death.

Below is a sample of my survey of five God-sized questions, where my job was not to "listen to reply" but "listen to hear." What do *you* hear, in Bill's answers?

Bill is a stable man in his fifties, well educated. He was not afraid of me or my faith talk. His worldview could be summed up: "What's good for you is great, what's good for me is great, and that's what makes the world go round." He agreed to take the survey when I told him that my only role was to listen to him and see if I could hear what he was saying. It put him in the driver's seat. I wasn't setting him up, and he respected that and believed it to be true.

Question #1
Where do you believe the world came from?

When I first asked the question, Bill went through an elaborate scientific explanation: "Evolution and science holds the only real answer out there." He went into genetics, the vastness of time, the discoveries in Africa, and even such things as Carbon-14 dating. Bill said that there is only one good answer, and that's evolution and the survival of the fittest. I wrote all this down and asked if he had anything else to say.

He began to speak about Darwin, the Galapagos Islands, and the Smithsonian Museum of Natural History in DC. He then talked about Stephen Hawkings, who said, "God not only plays dice; He also sometimes throws the dice where they cannot be seen." Hmmmm, I thought. Then Bill said, "Even if there is only one possible unified theory, it is just a set of rules and equations. What is it that breathes fire into the equations and makes a universe for them to describe?" He told me, "There is no heaven or afterlife for broken-down computers; that is a fairy story for people afraid of the dark." I said to Bill, "This is very valuable, got anything else?" He said, "No, that's it, Al. What's the next question?" But before I could present Question #2, Bill commented, "But you know, where the *first* matter came from is a crazy puzzle for the mind, isn't it, Al?"

"Sure is, Bill," I said. I had a promise to keep: I was only listening.

Question #2
What do you believe about God?

"Wow," Bill said, "you don't play around, do you?" He launched into some questions of his own. "What makes you think there is a God? Does he speak from a cloud, or jump out when you're in the forest or something? Ha ha. Does he look like George Burns or Morgan Freeman? You know all the wars of the world seem to be about whose God is bigger, you know? And by the way, you Christians aren't exempt from killing people and starting fights because people don't believe." Bill paused, and then he asked the real question. "Where *is* God, as my wife is now in her second bout with cancer? Al, why would God do that to such a good woman and mother? Go ask your God that question, Al, and let me know what he says, would you? I'm done with this question, Al."

Question #3
What do you believe about Jesus Christ?

"Hmmmm. You know, my mom was a Christian, and she would pray around the table at dinner. My dad thought it was nuts, but he didn't mind either. He said he couldn't

138

close his eyes at prayer in case someone stole his dinner. Ha ha. Mom wore a cross around her neck; it was gold and we buried her in it. Jesus likely lived and was real, but all those miracles like healing the blind and sick, well, it's a stretch. You believe that stuff, Al? Oh, that's right, you can't say anything. Smart man. All I know is, a big fuss is made at Christmas and Easter, he must be real to somebody. Crosses kind of creep me out, because bad things happened on them, right?"

"Anything else Bill?"

"Yeah. How can this Jesus help my sick wife?"

Question #4
What do you believe about life after death?

"Well," he paused. "My mom's in heaven. She believed it and lived it. I can't imagine her not getting in. My dad and me, that's another story."

"Bill, can I ask an unfair question?"

"Sure, why stop now?"

"If there is a heaven, would you want your kids to be there with your mom?"

Long pause. "Is this almost over, Al?"

"No Bill, I have questions that will keep us here to next Monday, ha ha!"

"I don't have a good answer for you, Al. I'm not gonna cry."

"Oops, too late, Bill."

"I hate you Al." Bill's body language was suddenly less confident, shrinking as if a hidden sorrow had been pinched.

"I know you do, and that's why we're friends, Bill, haha. We are almost done; let's get through this last question, Bill."

Question #5
If you could ask God one question, what would it be?

"Are you real? How can I come to believe in something I can't see? If you are real, why are things so hard here on earth? Why did all those people die in 9/11 in such a horrible way?"

"Anything else Bill?"

"No. Maybe — how's my mom doing?"

* * *

This interview with Bill shows that people are alive in the Image of God. An active search is going on, in the secret places of their minds and hearts. The unchurched may wear sunglasses, hiding their souls from untrusted speakers. Inside, they may be wishing that someone would ask them about that scar that cannot tan, and how it came to be. Or hoping someone will read the cryptic messages in their tattoos.

But the Judeo-Christian Ethic that undergirds much of what we think and say is now in a museum. Maybe it's not even in a display case, for tourists to point to as being a real relic. It actually might be in storage *underneath* the museum, alongside Teddy Roosevelt's cavalry sword.

Yet the Image of God is alive and well. It wants to be discovered, and craves a relationship. We can see the wonder of that image in the person we are talking to! God is bigger, multidimensional. It is breathtaking to discover His very being in the person in front of us.

If the Image of God were to write a blues song to us, what would that Image say?

> For these things I weep;
> My eyes run down with water;
> Because far from me is a comforter,
> One who restores my soul.

— Lamentations 1:16

Chapter 9

The Resurrection of Sabbath

The soul that loves God has its rest in God and in God
alone. In all the paths that men walk in in the world,
they do not attain peace until they draw nigh to hope
in God.
— St. Isaac the Syrian, Homily 56, 89

During my years as a pastor, my Sunday mornings were
full of highs and lows. Most Sundays I enjoyed preaching;
the text meant something to my own soul, and sometimes I
would finally "get" the text in the midst of my sermon. But
whenever someone said, "Great sermon, Pastor," although
I was pleased at the compliment, I knew that this might be
the hidden signal of a difficult coffee meeting ahead.

Each week, I entered into at least 20 conversations about
people's stories and their hurts. I appreciated the sacred
space into which people invited me, and I sensed God's
pleasure when I sought to understand the difficulties, or
even chaos, of their lives. A marriage on the rocks, a bad
medical result, a child suspended, a pink slip, a crisis of
faith — difficult circumstances that always prompted some
version of the question: "Is the Bible true and the way to
go?"

There were also the hard Sundays of conflicts over whose
job it should be to fix a leaking roof, or teach the adult ed
classes, or pay the mortgage, or fix the sound system. And
I got used to the debater who would wait for the sermon to

143

end and then somehow block my path to the back door. On other Sundays I was not reformed enough, as someone would tell me, or I told stories that went on too long, or I didn't make the gospel plain enough. The hard part was, my critics were usually right.

The children were always a delight. I loved the little boy who called me "Aster Pal" instead of pastor Al. I loved doing children's sermons, giving one simple, easy-to-swallow message, and I knew that it was the adults who would benefit the most — including me.

So being a pastor has always been a calling in my life and one I have delighted in, though at times (I confess) I have wondered whether something else was waiting around the corner. But each time Monday morning arrived, I was always pretty tired, pushing down feelings of depression, anger, and a desire to be completely and utterly alone.

My usual solution was to load my 100-pound chocolate lab into the truck (with 400,000 crazy trip miles already on it) and head to the river. Harley never cared about my sermons, or about what I was wearing, or about my state of mind or whether or not I was a Christian, or how tired I was. Just the sight or sound of my arrival sent his body into leaping delight. His tail was a rubber whip that you treated with respect. The possibility that I might throw him a ball evoked uncontrollable dancing — and all the better if I would send that ball 300 feet into the flood rapids of the Potomac.

Once, coming back from speaking in Philadelphia, I pulled into a spot along the Susquehanna River, near Route 95.

Harley was in my truck; he travels everywhere with me, as long as it doesn't get too hot. I parked at a remote section of the river and opened the back hatch, and Harley leaped out as if this was his last adventure in this life. Picking up on his enthusiasm, I grabbed the tennis racket and hit the rubber ball as hard and far as I could, into the river.

Then I noticed a couple of things. The river was flood stage, and the January temperature was about 27 degrees. As big as he was, I saw Harley get swept away immediately in the fast water. I didn't panic, but the thought crossed my mind that this might be the time he didn't come back to me. And how would I explain this to all the Harley fans in my life?

I waited a long 35 minutes, as sadness came over me. I thought about making a second cup of coffee on the propane stove. And then I saw the tiny brown dot, way off in the distance, running straight at me. It was Harley, I could not mistake his locomotion. But as he got closer I saw he had become a frozen sculpture in motion — each hair was now encased in ice. As he got closer it began to crack, the ice shedding off of his fur. And — he had the ball. Harley placed that round reward at my feet and then stared intently in my face, to signal, "Let's do it again!" And we did! I threw that ball five more times before leaving the river. Harley slept all the way home, preparing for the next outing. Clearly, Harley *got* the Sabbath.

Exodus 20:8-11 reads:

> Remember the Sabbath day, to keep it holy. Six days you shall labor, and do all your work, but the

seventh day is a Sabbath to the Lord your God. On it you shall not do any work, you, or your son, or your daughter, your male servant, or your female servant, or your livestock, or the sojourner who is within your gates. For in six days the Lord made heaven and earth, the sea, and all that is in them, and rested on the seventh day. Therefore the Lord blessed the Sabbath day and made it holy.

This sacred Sabbath has become a lost delight, this badly-needed source of recovery for our souls. We never rest our bodies and souls from the insecurities, loneliness, and labors that seem to imprison them. Sabbath can replace these burdens with a time of simple play that can make our hearts sing.

Observation and remembrance of Sabbath is one of the Ten Commandments. Implicit in the definition of Sabbath is "re-creation," or the recreation of the mind and soul. It's a day of worship: seeing God's worth and letting that knowledge feed your own particular soul, in a real, knowable, and particular way. What was my particular Sabbath? For any pastor, the church is the place of work rather than of rest or recreation, and it also had its own kinds of stress for me. The organ music in high Church worship settings, for example, creates a stress inside of me: I neither liked it nor felt God's presence in that music. So, each Monday, I found myself retreating again and again to the river with Harley for a few hours, never able to get enough — of what? Enough Sabbath to rest; enough play to fill my soul with the wonder of God's presence in creation.

God walks in His garden with us

Genesis 3 gives us insights into the ways of God with His children. It reads, "Then the man and his wife heard the sound of the Lord God, as he was walking in the garden in the cool of the day." No doubt God enjoyed walking in the beautiful garden he had spoken into existence. But He especially loved walking with Adam and Eve. We can let our imaginations wander a bit and ask, *what did that walk look like?* I think God's creation gives us hints into just how God longs to walk with us.

Did you ever see a grandpa walking with his five-year-old granddaughter as she chatters away, holding his two fat fingers and delighting in the safety of this big old joke-telling man she calls "Poppy"? Ever see a teenager walk his brand new, scent-crazed puppy in a park in the springtime? Ever see a mother duck cross the road, with her fast-footed brood of seven small ducklings behind her? Ever see a professor, hands clasped behind his back, as he walks with a freshman student on campus, listening to questions he's heard 500 times, while offering fresh ears? Ever see God our father, in the garden with Adam and Eve, listening as He walks to the toucans and monkeys calling in the tree tops? Have you ever pictured *yourself* walking in God's presence, as you live in the particular thing that delights your soul?

Perhaps Sabbath is truly the way forward, in our next season of evangelism. We are not "present" with other people, when God hasn't filled the void in our own soul. St. Basil the Great said, "As it is impossible to verbally describe the sweetness of honey to one who has never tasted honey, so the goodness of God cannot be clearly communicated by way of teaching, if we ourselves are not able to penetrate into the goodness of the Lord by our own experience." (Conversations on the Psalms, 29.) I believe that Sabbath rest is the care the evangelist so desperately needs as he reaches out to others. Our souls are tired and lonely, and they long for a walk with God alone.

People today are surrounded by noise of all kinds; they have their ears assaulted by a fire siren, as they seek to navigate the noise of the social media revolution. Psychologists are now developing terms for people who have lost touch with what is real, who have an impaired ability to separate the virtual from the actual. What do vacation planners advertise in their commercials? *Quiet places* for minds and souls. Car manufacturers describe the "car's cabin" as a safety zone shutting out noise and pollution, as you are serenaded by high definition stereo in gridlock traffic. Spas are inventing ways to quiet the noise of our world and our hearts. In this noisy world, noisy souls are looking for someone quiet they can talk with. Can the evangelist be that quiet person?

Centuries ago, the monastic movement understood the problem of noise. Theirs is the art of listening and hearing. The broader Christian church has dismissed the monastic way because it can't be quantified; and, yes, it was a broken system, like every other system run by broken men. But there is value in it as well, benefits that we need desperately today. Cameron Diaz put it, "You haven't partied until you've partied at dawn in complete silence with Buddhist monks."

I think it is safe to say that we have become a noise-filled people; our interior lives are often chaotic and messy. We are all about doing, memorizing, systematizing, and planning, but not walking with God and simply being in His mysterious, fulfilling presence. How can we listen to others, if *we* are not listened to? How can our listening break into *hearing*, if we don't feel that God is hearing the whispers and the fragile fears of our own souls? How can we hear the noise that is so threatening for others, if the background noise in our own life is not quieted — with God — in Sabbath rest?

The problem of noise only becomes magnified when, in our uneasy spiritual state, we try to offer to the unchurched a Gospel proposal. Let me be careful here: *we do not have to be perfect*. Can God use any dull tool to start faith in a soul? Can He use a skull-and-bones tattoo on a grandma to awaken eternity in a heart? Yes, He can! But I believe that what He likes using as well is a quiet soul, one that can be simply present with whoever is ready to come into the kingdom, whether sooner or later. And perhaps the way forward, for our next generation of listening and hearing soul-winners, is for us to resurrect, for ourselves, a precious Sabbath rest.

For many people, Sabbath has come to mean trying to keep yet another set of rules one day a week, rules that we often break and pretend we don't. That pretense can build up inside us like a scary ice dam on the Susquehanna in

January. Maybe we should think of keeping Sabbath as an art form rather than a set of rules. It's up to each of us to learn how best to recreate ourselves and restore our own inner peace, to be equal to the difficult task we have set ourselves.

I've been thinking a lot about Sabbath rest lately, due to a freak accident that actually prevented me from talking for about three weeks. I had been fishing for 12 hours on the Chesapeake Bay, without thinking too much about taking care of myself. I became deeply dehydrated, and on the way home I began to vomit in the truck. My friend, who was driving, stopped at the side of the highway and I stepped outside. My last memory was telling myself, "Don't fall into traffic!" I hit the concrete face first and woke up in the ambulance, with unbearable pain in my jaw: both hinges and my chin were broken.

Who would believe this story? Not the doctors, who wanted to know what *really* happened. Then I met my surgeon, a specialist named Dr Z. His words, tone, and body language said clearly, "I am so sorry Mr. Dayhoff, so sorry." His very human empathy gave me the energy to open myself to the adventure that lay ahead, and his work inspired empathy in me as well. There was grace all around me, filling my soul has been with the empathy and care from my wife, my loving blues buddies, from my mom asking me to "describe the pain," as if she felt it herself, wherever it was. Their empathy switched something deep in me — from focusing on my fear and guarding my manhood, to being able to receive the well-chosen words and the care of those dear to me.

After the first surgery, the swelling nearly closed off my ear canals completely. My jaw was wired shut and my ears were all but useless. I could watch what others were doing, and hear them if they shouted. I was closed for business. But my core became activated, my powers of observation increased. I found a great new joy in the nearness of my wife, who served me hand and foot, and in the empathy shown by Dr Z. and all of my hugging, soup-making blues buddies; life had become a big, BIG joy. And my soul needed quiet to get there. What else had changed? Can I be honest? Maybe the best kind of evangelism I was capable of came in those difficult weeks: God had wired my jaw shut! Wired-shut became my sanctuary; God was in it. I started *hearing*.

Another confession: I worried what jaw surgery would do to my face. Would it turn into a "no" face? A perpetual scowl? I could see my blues buddies staring at my face, after they heard the gruesome details. Then Gary put his finger on it. "You know, Pastor Al, you might be left with a permanent smirk!" I laughed out loud and joked, "Sure, it's how I always look at you!" But inside I was mortified. Left with a smirk? I started to look at the faces around me — the "yes" faces, the "no" faces. Well, maybe this made some kind of sense. The pastor is the one with the *smirk* face. Could it be that my new jaw, and face, and mangled diction are building my empathy, giving me a clearer eye to discover the blues people that God has brought into my life?

Or maybe it's God's way of teaching me to listen. A second lengthy surgery has gifted me with a synthetic jaw socket;

now, every time I speak, my ears pick up the squeak of the Teflon and titanium. "Al, whenever you hear the squeak, don't talk, just *listen*."

Breaking one's jaw is probably not the best way to regain the Sabbath experience, but it was a powerful one for me. Being forced to listen and not talk, forced to depend on the love and the kindness of others; feeling gratitude for the healing power of the body, and for the care of a gifted surgeon. Having more time to reflect than we ever allow ourselves. However our Sabbath comes, it is a time for the core to be quieted, experiencing the presence of God and being fully welcomed into mystery. Our souls are noisy — in the Christian community just as everywhere else. Evangelism needs to be more like yoga. When we stop trying to muscle through the moment with our techniques, the Sabbath will radiate God's presence in ways we can't ever measure.

> Happiness is a pure heart, for such a heart becomes the throne of God. . . . What can be lacking to them? Nothing, nothing at all! For they have the greatest good in their hearts: God Himself!
>
> — St. Nektarios of Aegina,
> *Path to Happiness*, 1

Chapter 10

Where do we go from here?

Don't you have a saying, "It's still four months until harvest"? I tell you, open your eyes and look at the fields! They are ripe for harvest.

— John 4: 35

I hope that this book offers some new revelations for our day and age, as we live out the great commission together. Maybe we can revisit some timeless truths framed in a new voice, or in new lyrics we can hear and trust.

I believe it is possible that we are at the onset of a wave of new conversions. Those coming to faith might surprise us all — conversions as surprising as the methods God chooses and anoints. In this chapter, I share some thoughts about how we can reshape our methods to meet our opportunities.

Stop talking

One Sunday in the blues bar, I asked one of my new friends what he thought of church people. His answer was immediate: "If you would all just *shut the hell up* you might learn something." Ouch. Another phrase I have grown accustomed to hearing is, "Today, nobody listens to anybody." People are just waiting their turn to jump in the conversation and present their side.

I was raised by parents who were about 22 years apart in age (Benny Goodman meets the Rolling Stones?). I love both of my parents, but as I remember it, each of them sort of talked in the direction of the other person, or maybe to someone else as if referring to the other person; they rarely talked directly to each other. One day it dawned on me that I was just like them. Inside the Christian mind, like most people, as we listen to someone else talking we are always framing a response — a *yeah, but*! That "*yeah, but*" steals our hearing, shuts down communication, stops empathy.

Real empathy conveys a feeling of being cared for that goes beyond any doctrine; it begins with a genuine interest in the other person's story. Our "*yeah, but*" lives in our apologetics — an excellent discipline, but one that has its own limits. "*Yeah, but*" lives in a superiority complex, in the arrogance that comes with having too much knowledge and too little self-awareness of our own secret idols. When someone in my seminar asks, "But Al, when do I speak back?" I answer: "When they *ask* you to" — and that might take six months or more.

A conversation is not ten or twenty minutes of talking in a doorway. It takes place over months and years, as the relationship and faith discussion and "listening to hear" play out. We earn the right to speak through being quiet — soul-deep quiet, honest about our own struggle with suffering and waiting to be asked our opinion. That is when we can weave our own words with people's real stories.

Evangelism: fishing expedition and laboratory

I have shared with you my love of fishing. But I'm just a rookie: I stand next to the real fishermen and try to imitate them, and sometimes I get to take the rod when they have a fish and reel it in.

What I have learned from the real fishermen is their passion for everything involved in fishing. They love the smell of salt water, the sound of the surf, the whirr of the 225 hp motor at full throttle. They have 48 different lures, and they can catch their own bait in the surf. They love sharpening their filet knives and getting a sunburn from the water. I recently saw one angler catch a sea trout, slowly feel the side of his body and ponder the artwork of his neon colors. It was a magic moment as he then released him back for another day. He whispered something to the fish: I think he said, "See you next year, buddy." Evangelism might be best lived in a fishing boat, pondering the head winds, the type of fish at hand, the fickleness of a certain species, like the pull of a fighting blues caught in New England in the fall. Let's take sheer delight in the moment, in the never-to-be-replicated setting — *and in the fish.* From so many years of pastoring, I realize that the ever-present question below the surface was always simply, "Does Pastor Al *like* me?"

Every time he sees me, my buddy Chuck says, "Al, you're not gonna convert me today." Honestly, I have never tried! So, who *is* it who's talking to Chuck? What glorious thing is happening, in the birthline inside his soul? *Methinks he doth protest too much.* And, by the way, he does know how much I like him.

There are some days when our gospel proposals bring home souls through Jesus alone and into the Kingdom. There are ripe, God-anointed intersections, where a soul sees the way to heaven through coming to God in private prayer. And there are days of disappointment, too. Our work is not simple or automatic. I think of it as a kind of working laboratory. We need to feel free to look and laugh at our own hang-ups, to try something different, to step on a landmine or two, or to have absolutely no success for days or even weeks.

One of my dear blues buddies looked me in the eyes, and I knew that a dance step was coming — a lead and follow, the question-answer dance. The twist was always, could I discover the back narrative, the question they really wanted to ask. And the question came: "Pastor Al are we just a bunch of lab rats for you?" I thought for a moment before I answered. "Absolutely," I said. "And I am to you, my friend. See if this stuff is working for me, too, that's fair." Her eyes were still mildly suspicious, but also still my friend.

Spiritual conversations

I was sitting in the waiting room of Merchant's Tire & Auto Center. You know, the one with *Tires Today* magazines for recreational reading, while your car is put through a CT scan to reveal that everything is broken? I looked up and saw a Buddhist monk, wearing the distinctive orange, wrapped robe and leather sandals and smooth head, walking from his car toward the glass front door of Merchants. The guys behind the counter saw him, too, and one of them said, "God, don't look now but here comes the Dalai Lama." The monk opened the door and went up to the counter. His accent was strong, probably Vietnamese, I thought. I pretended to read my "Adventures in Tires" article.

The monk said, "I need new tires."

Bubba answered him, "We don't do re-tires here."

"You sell tires?"

Bubba answered, loudly and slowly, "We are not hiring anyone right now." It was killing me. Even though I wanted to sit and watch this comedy, I stepped in to help the conversation. "Our friend needs new tires."

"Well, why didn't he say so?"

I grinned. "We aren't very smart on this side of the counter, you know?" Bubba handed the clipboard to my new friend. We had a great chat as we sat in the waiting room, and a week later he stopped by the church to talk.

Interpreting, I recently understood, is how I have lived my life. Instead of hearing what people say, I seem to be wired to hear what's behind their words. Growing up in a chaotic home, I came to expect that from one second to the next, a cherished family memory could be transformed into a lifelong wound inflicted by harsh, angry words. I needed to develop radar and feelers to know what to expect at any moment. Lots of other people I meet have this orientation, and many don't. Nobody gets the whole package to navigate this rodeo of life. We all must all learn to trust and rely on others' gifts to get us through the confusion.

Listening to the unchurched, I tend to hear the Image of God speaking. If all of us are made in the image of God, that Image can't stop bubbling out. We all have our guarded moments, when we choose each word perfectly, and we have unguarded moments when the soul speaks from somewhere else. That "somewhere" can be — and is — the image of God. When our bodies hurt, when we watch a sunset or attend a funeral, or when we go fishing or mold clay in pottery class, our souls bubble to the surface. Hearing the spiritual conversations in those moments, we can see the image of God in the unbeliever, a source of growing respect and excitement in the listening evangelist.

But can we hear spiritual conversations, or only religious ones? In the church we have a language, a culture, a way of thinking and being that has become real barrier to hearing what a non-Christian is saying to us. I realized recently that I am an EQ (emotional intelligence) guy in an IQ denomination. IQ hears facts and can process great volumes of information, something I have been jealous of my whole life. EQ uses different eyes, ears, and processors. In my Presbyterian denomination, we value doctrine, and systems of doctrine, and systems to systematize our doctrine. We have conferences on what I call the outer wrapper of theology, those systems that absorb our attention before we can get to the actual doctrine.

Expect divine appointments

Kung Fu was an American action-adventure western drama series starring David Carradine; the series aired on ABC from October, 1972, to April, 1975, for a total of 63 episodes. (I loved this show almost as much as the The Wild, Wild West with Robert Conrad, who wielded incredible gadgets and slept on a moving train.) Kung Fu was based on a simple, unencumbered philosophy of life. You simply walked the earth. That's right: you would encounter the things you are meant to experience, the people you are supposed to meet, and the dangers that will shape what you are meant to be. Kung Fu had one providential experience after another — fighting the bad guys, assisting the desperate, and living in the tension of each appointed resolution.

Could it be that God has designed divine appointments in our weeks and days, and it is up to us to be available to them? Once, when I had finally given up all that terrible fast food from McDonald's, I was sitting in the late night drive-through of Burger King. The speaker was silent; I imagined that the kids at the work-stations were looking at me through the camera and drawing mustaches on the screen. I finally walked up to the window. It was a middle-aged woman, not a kid, and she was visibly upset. I asked her what was wrong. She said, "My babysitter just called, and my little boy fell down the stairs." I asked her if I could pray for him. Yes, she said, his name is Juan. I said a fast-food prayer and got my food, as she asked the next person, "Can I help you?" She gave me a smile of thanks, holding her hand on her heart.

Brothers and sisters, can you imagine a life designed by God, where divine appointments that are created in eternity can come about in fast food drive-throughs? Maybe we need to be constantly living in the expectation of what God might be up to today — in and through me — in the present.

Evangelize the evangelist

It is not only the unchurched who need us to be "present." True, we need to spend time with them and hear their hurts, and much later we can give our proposal. We must let listening give way to hearing. And, in this same gentle way, we need to be encouraging to the tired, frightened, beaten-down evangelists working alongside us. Writing this book is, more than anything else, a way to give new respect and space to the individuals who will lead this new charge. Many capable Christians are sitting at the door of souls coming into heaven, and they, too, need help.

As a pastor for nearly 25 years, I know the difficulties well. The landmines hidden on the ground, in our own souls, and in the wounded are always ready to explode, often enough to send us into full retreat. So, we run to hide behind our doctrine, our pulpits, our church culture, our intellectualism — our strike-before-being-struck style of talking. I get it: it's a rodeo of scrapes, burns, and stings. Many of us are in full evangelism retreat, at most inviting one or two souls to Easter service.

So, I honor and appreciate those who took their posts in the past, in the world of evangelism. Those who labored in their way and on their watch should be saluted and

160

hugged. We should love our pastors who gave up much, as did their families, to spend their lives telling the message that Jesus saves sinners. Dear ones, let's evangelize the evangelists; they have much work to get done, and we can learn from all of them.

Study forgiveness

Unforgiven is a 1992 Western produced and directed by Clint Eastwood. It's a sordid story of gunslingers, pimps, prostitutes, bullies, and seemingly innocent people. The theme comes in through many windows: gunslingers and others who carry horrible weights that are simply never forgiven. But life must go on, scores must be evened and responsibilities fulfilled. The unforgiven seek to hide, but never well enough.

Once a man asked me, "If Adam had run to God in the garden after eating of the tree of knowledge of good and evil and pleaded for God's forgiveness, would it have been granted?" I said that I didn't know, but it was a great question. I do know that Adam hid, knowing the shame of his nakedness and thinking, somehow, that he was actually hiding from God. But God asked the question "Where are you?" It was God who gave Adam ears to listen, the mind to hear, and a voice to answer with intelligence. Adam was saying, "I'm hiding in fear, shame, and the sense of needing forgiveness."

People today are walking around "unforgiven," seeking the help in alcohol, food, porn, or whatever addiction can mask the pain. Others serve mean and deceptive taskmasters — idols of power, money, success, or

161

whatever gives us validation. Ronnie said to me at a blues bar, "I cry often over the eight babies I aborted because I didn't want to pay child support. I dream about them and they talk to me in my dreams and nightmares." Another woman told me that her son was murdered after she asked him to go to the store to get groceries. These are people who can never forgive themselves.

We need to understand what bedevils and torments our current and future converts. We need to join their journey by knowing their sorrow, grasping the weight they carry around as the unforgiven. Yes, Jesus saves sinners. Most of my delightful blues buddies know that they're sinners — just ask them (but ask nicely!). When you tell them that there is the possibility of walking, sleeping, and living free of guilt and in *forgiveness*, they will hold you with their tired eyes. Let's develop a new awareness of the unforgiven who live and walk among us.

Go to your blues bar

I quickly understood that the blues bar folks would come into my home, but never to my church. I felt it as a slap in the face, but this meant something important. Some of them called it a place of hypocrites: "I already *know* I'm one; why join others?" Others were afraid of judgment — "Lightening will strike!" — and others of being overly marketed — "That's a sales booth, and once you enter you can never get out." Some held grudges from deep in the past: "My grandfather said he would never, ever go back even when he died; he wanted to be buried in a funeral home only."

Whatever the excuses, they are telling us that we have to venture outside the church and go to our "blues bar." Maybe that's going to be a knitting gathering, a sci-fi movie club, a car race, or a dance. And this is their territory, not ours. We are there to be open, available for friendships, curious about the other people who are made in God's image. Watch God unfold a divine appointment, as you befriend people, laugh with them, and invite them to your home. Go visit your own "blues bar," and go with a prayerful expectation of divine appointments.

Become the parish priest of your blues bar, bowling league, running club, pottery class. Don't go in order to evangelize; become one of the group — and watch your blues bar meet for church.

We are in new territory

If I try to tell you that something is changing that is bigger than we can detect, you will probably just yawn, "Really?" We are all overwhelmed with the volume of information coming at us every day. As we struggle to pay our mortgages, we also experience the increasing mix of cultures and economies, the shift of power from the West to the East, the world becoming less married and more single, the Western birthrate dropping to 1.3 children, the faith pluralism so many embrace in order not to be an oddball.

Is there an answer? I propose that we begin our own journey to be "present." And I think that we can learn something from Alcoholics Anonymous about the process of change. (1) Work for progress, not perfection. Perfection means having a ready reply; progress means just being able to *hear*. (2) People need some kind of "sponsor," and in AA, the sponsor is someone who has been there too. Our own rediscovery of the answers to the five questions will enable us to sponsor another soul seeking faith. (3) The AA Serenity Prayer captures the journey toward progress:

> God, give me grace to accept with serenity
> the things that cannot be changed,
> Courage to change the things
> which should be changed,
> and the Wisdom to distinguish
> the one from the other.
> Living one day at a time,
> Enjoying one moment at a time,
> Accepting hardship as a pathway to peace,
> Taking, as Jesus did,
> This sinful world as it is,
> Not as I would have it,
> Trusting that You will make all things right,
> If I surrender to Your will,
> So that I may be reasonably happy in this life,
> And supremely happy with You forever in the next.
> Amen.

Is there a prayer we can share with all of our friends — seekers, nonseekers, non-Christians? I invite you to share your ideas. Meanwhile, I would like to share my own prayer of progress:

God meet me where I am, help me with my challenges. Show me you are real, in your time and in my space. Help me to help others believe, trust and discover your promises, as others help me in my journey of faith. Amen

I offer the five questions of Chapter 8 as tools for a "sponsor" to use, as a way of giving a few other souls hearing and empathy. We all need to listen to the hurts and wounds of the people God has positioned in our lives; and we need to wait for hearing to happen. It is only then that, when asked, we can communicate to them the timeless truth, that Jesus saves sinners like you and me, forever and ever. Amen and Amen.

Epilogue: The Steps We Can Take Now

There are steps that each of us can begin to take, *today*, to work toward a more effective evangelism.

1 Spend our young men and women better.

Let's encourage some of our new church planters to spend about 18 months doing intentional evangelism research, by talking to people *outside* the church and hearing what they say. Our seminary students are best positioned to be the CT scan on our culture, to do the fieldwork to discover where people really are. We are wasting their talents, if we steer them only to the classroom and the library to be credentialed. *Let's unleash a new season of evangelism apprenticeships.* Encourage our doctor of ministry students to do extensive fieldwork with non-Christians, using the five questions.

2 Invest in our own process of discovery.

Spend the same amount of energy, thought, and money as we spend on our building, on our intentional evangelism ideas and experiments. (If we build it, they won't necessarily come!) Shift our priorities away from our building projects, long ordination periods, and theological precision to more meaningful evangelism and fieldwork.

3 Understand and accept mocking.

Within the mocking of the non-Christian there is also a search for authentic relationship. When we are defensive, we are no longer in the moment.

4 Get ready (or get cynical).

Coming to terms with our new world means preparation and mental readiness. Cynicism uses up the energy needed for the evangelist's adventures in a new changing world.

5 Create outposts.

The only people coming in to our church buildings are transfers, not converts. We are now empty nesters, after the kids have left the house. Our outposts can be a blues bar, swing dance club, bowling team, Boy Scout troop, knitting circle, or a country club — any group that needs a "parish priest." Will the bowling league people eventually come into the church? Maybe — but don't count on it.

6 Share the load.

Let's not do what we often do — put the whole load on our pastors. Help to shoulder the mission without needing credit, with money, prayers, and sacrifice.

7 Harness the power of five central questions.

I am a lover of deep education, but it does not it take a Ph.D. to share a powerful conversation with a non-Christian. We do not need to do the talking in every conversation. We can ask the big questions and then listen to *hear* — not to reply.

Question 1: Where do you believe the world came from?

Question 2: What do you believe about God?

Question 3: What do you believe about Jesus Christ?

Question 4: What do you believe about life after death?

Question 5: If you could ask God one question, what would it be?

I invite you to explore these five questions in one of my workshops, along with other dedicated people who are seeking ways to fulfill their personal mission in Christ. Each workshop leads me to ponder, "Lord how are you going to work in our lives today?"

Acknowledgements

I thank, first of all, my ever-serving, unstoppable, art-passionate wife, who loves me and wakes to see if I'm sleeping okay. Our love adventure is 35 years old and growing, and I'm ready for the highs and lows to come, as long as we do it together. I love you, Deb.

I thank my mentoring children, Erin and Wesley, who love being alive, laugh at my jokes, and teach me who Jesus is. (Oh, the fun still to come!)

I owe great thanks to my parents, Al and Hope Dayhoff: Mom, you were the first blues singer in my life, and Dad, you said it would all be better in the morning. I'm just now beginning to get it.

To Chris Labs and Harry Watt, our ET board members, who mentor me with sage advice, Olympic-size self-deprecating humor, and deep life friendship. Let's fish, smoke cigars, and repeat.

To Lauren Bleam, who took a very active and effective role in shaping this book and welcomed in others. And to the faithful readers who gave her their insights and valuable feedback on each chapter.

To my dear blues buddies (way too many to list!) who have loved me, fed and wined me at their tables, told me preacher jokes I could either choke on or laugh at. Thank you for allowing me to sit with you, dance with you, and receive healing hugs from you. Let's never stop dancing, here and in the next world. I love you.

To Brian Hamilton, Pastor of Westminster Presbyterian Church in Washington DC. You have taught me to look for the unseen person. You introduced me to the subtle complexities of racism, poverty, and a church of humans like me seeking their way in this crazy world. Your flock has loved me, I felt its realness. When I asked the group of elderly ladies with hats "Can I join your club," you all said, "You're already in!" Please never end Blue Monday — it's part of my life.

To Clare Wolfowitz: you are a gift my friend. You are the master of "dance like no one is watching." Your patience with me as you edit, adapting to fit into my thoughts, intents and trajectory, makes me let down my guard. I can see new colors, hear new music, and delight in blues lyrics that hit bone deep.

To the blues musicians, some who are listed in this book and some I know only as the drummer or bass player at a blues jam. You are playing God's music, describing the weight of a cursed and a vice-gripped world that can be oh-so-cruel. I strangely feel encouragement from your sound and the lyrics that speak it as it is.

To Blue Church: let's grow from inside the bar and reach outward. We can still be a church that meets in a blues bar — and also a blues bar that meets for church. New followers of Jesus have that "new car smell" that makes me smile and give me hope.

About the Author

Rev. Allan Dayhoff is the Founder and Executive Director of Evangelize Today, an evangelical outreach organization that offers a pioneering one- to three-day seminar, designed to give participants the opportunity to reflect on their own conversion process and to apply those insights. More information can be found at www.evangelizetoday.info.

He also serves as Senior Pastor of Grace Fellowship Church, which he founded in 1992. He previously headed Dayhoff Construction.

Rev. Dayhoff earned a Doctor of Ministries at Covenant Theological Seminary in St. Louis, MO. He wrote his dissertation on "Confrontational Monologue vs. Relational Dialogue, as it Relates to the Image of God in the Non-Christian and the Transfer of Faith."

Praise for *Church in a Blues Bar* and *Evangelize Today*

Apologetics, the ability to "give a word back," begins *not* with talking but with *listening to hear* — that is, treating my fellow *imago dei* (image of God) bearer with dignity and respect. "Giving a word back" begins with realizing that life for many for our fellow imago dei bearers is not a life of "living happily ever after"; rather, life has dealt many of our neighbors an awfully "bad hand." So, this book asks (and answers) the question, "How do I show respect and dignity to my fellow imago bearer?" Answer: "Tarry long in listening — *with your hand over your mouth.*"

> Dr. Luke Bobo, BBT Curriculum Director
> & Resident Theologian; a former Director
> of the Francis Schaeffer Institute,
> Covenant Theological Seminary, St. Louis,
> MO

The core gospel is always there. What Al does, like a skilled travel guide, is to take us on a journey of re-discovery of too-familiar territory. What we hear as "new" is actually quite old, so old we forgot we knew it: that God not only loves the people he has made, he sort of *likes* them. And then God invites us to join Him in his affection for people — and to follow the path of affection into respectful listening and truth telling. Al, like the Holy Spirit, catalyzes affection and respect for people. Al's seminar is a special gift.

> Rev. Tory K. Baucum, Rector
> Truro Anglican Church

I wanted you all to know about a new ministry called *Evangelize Today* that I am very excited about. . . . I went through one of these workshops and it revolutionized my understanding of evangelism and gave me some great tools for becoming more consistent in my own life.

Rev. Tom Herrick, Executive Director
Titus Church Planting

I recently attended a day-long *Evangelize Today* seminar, hosted and facilitated by Rev. Al Dayhoff. The first step in that process was an introspective look at my own life, from before I was born to the present — the good, the bad, and the ugly! Then, Al had me focus on my Christian walk, which did not start with the moment I first believed — it started when I was born, or even before I was born. Finally, Al showed us a way we could gently engage with someone on our heart, in a conversation about God that is not threatening in any way and produces some pretty amazing results! I found going through this process to be extremely edifying, opening doors to better evangelize to those I love, with a beautiful result which brought tears to my eyes. I most strongly recommend Al's training to any church interested in equipping and energizing its congregation!

Bob Tate, Executive Director
Truro Anglican Church

Over the course of over 40 years in full-time ministry, I have been through countless evangelism seminars and led a few myself; but none like *Evangelize Today*. ET stimulated my curiosity about others, to recognize our common human condition (suffering in a fallen world) and to see how that can be a bridge that ties our lives together and opens wide the door for Jesus to enter. This approach is especially appropriate to our postmodern world. I'd highly recommend it to anyone!

Larry Hoop
Original Vision Network
Coordinator of the PCA Original Vision
Ministries

We were looking for something that would really develop the average believer in Jesus Christ to be able to share their faith and have conversations that would develop within their network of friendships . . . The Evangelize Today Seminar really fits that particular model very, very, well.

Dr. Herb Ruby
Senior Pastor, Covenant of Grace Church